Gardens of Persia

Gardens of Persia
Penelope Hobhouse

Edited by Erica Hunningher
Photography by Jerry Harpur

KALES
PRESS

For my grandchildren,
Eleanor, Arthur, Anna, and Jack,
the travelers of the future.

Published in 2004 by Kales Press, Inc
Kenneth Kales, Publisher
Ken Wilson, Designer
Emily Hedges, Picture Researcher
Ruth Baldwin, Proofreader
Ken Wilson, Illustrator of Artwork and Garden Plans
Penny David, Indexer

Library of Congress Cataloging-in-Publication Data

Hobhouse, Penelope.
The Gardens of Persia / Penelope Hobhouse; edited by Erica
Hunningher; photography by Jerry Harpur.
p. cm.
Includes bibliographical references (p.).
ISBN 0-9670076-6-6 (hardcover : alk. paper)
1. Gardens, Persian. 2. Gardens--Iran. I. Hunningher, Erica. II.
Title.
SB458.5.H63 2004
712'.0955--dc21
2003014500

Typeset in Monotype Centaur
Printed and bound in Hong Kong

Kales Press, Inc
www.kalespress.com

◆ *A man digging,* ABOVE, *in a garden enclosed by a high wall with a large pine, a
cypress, flowering almonds and, possibly, a poplar. The miniature, painted in Shiraz in
1420, illustrates Ferdousi's 10th-century* Shahnameh. ◆ HALF TITLE *Miniature
from Nezami's* Khamseh, *painted in 1494 by Bihzad, showing a school set in a contemporary garden.* ◆ FRONTISPIECE *The Doulatabad Garden, Yazd.*

Contents

I	The elements of the Persian garden

"The Great King ... in all the districts he resides in and visits ... takes care that there are 'paradises' as they call them, full of all the good and beautiful things that the soil will produce." Xenophon *The Oeconomicus* 399 BC

 ON THE GREAT PLAIN OF MARV-DASHT EAST OF THE ZAGROS MOUNTAINS LIE THE SCATTERED remains of the earliest garden of which we have a record. Among the ruined foundations, set against a background of brown hills, gleaming white columns still soar into the sky and fragments of carvings are visible. Here, in a once fertile plain watered by the River Polvar northeast of Shiraz, Cyrus the Great, founder of the Achaemenid Empire, defeated the Medes near Pasargadae in 550 BC and, according to legend, decided to build his capital on the site of victory.

Cyrus was a political as well as a military genius. He established a united kingdom which his descendants developed into a mighty empire. His reign (558–528 BC) heralded a new civilization, a time of affluence and luxury, unheard of in previous eras, when gardens began to assume great importance in the cultural life of rulers. With a formal quadripartite groundplan, the garden Cyrus created 2,500 years ago is the oldest extant layout which can still be "read" and reconstructed, at least on paper, to provide tangible evidence of the origins of Persian gardens. Incorporating both architecture and planting, water rills and shade-giving pavilions, Cyrus's garden seems to offer the background to all later garden developments.

These first ideas of a garden as a paradise were to be as vital in the history of the spiritual Muslim garden and the Indian gardens of the Mughal Empire as they have been influential in the gardens of Renaissance Europe and Western civilization.

8

THE
ELEMENTS
OF THE
PERSIAN
GARDEN

ENCLOSED PARADISE

The buildings and gardens at Pasargadae formed an integrated composition, providing shade, vegetation, and a refuge. We do not have a contemporary description, but Cyrus the Great's garden will have had similar features to the 5th-century complex of palaces and pavilions belonging to Artaxerxes at the time of the invasion of Persia by Cyrus the Younger, satrap in Sardis. Described by Xenophon after 394 BC, this included gardens watered by an aqueduct—the earliest known record of gravity-fed water rills and basins arranged in a geometric system. The Spartan General Lysander, who joined Cyrus the Younger as a Greek mercenary in 401 BC, reported to Xenophon how the Persian kings excelled not only in war but also in gardening, creating *paradeisos* (paradises) where they collected plants, especially trees which bore fruit, and animals encountered during campaigns in foreign parts. Xenophon translated the Persian *pairidaeza* (a combination of *pairi* meaning "around" and *daeza* meaning "wall") into the Greek *paradeisos*, a term used for the Garden of Eden in Greek translations of the Bible. In modern Persian or Farsi the word *ferdous* means both paradise and garden.

Watercourses formed the principal axis and secondary axes of the main garden at Pasargadae. This geometric articulation of water channels meeting at right angles to divide the enclosure was based on the demands of fine stone construction for the irrigation canals and the need for periodic flooding, but the rills and wider basins were also decorative. After the first millennium, this four-fold theme was called a *chahar bagh* (*chahar* meaning "four" and *bagh* meaning "garden") and was to be the basis of later Persian garden design. The arrangement of channels, pools, transverse walks, terraces, and pavilions within a rectangular enclosure could be interpreted inside a courtyard for private or royal use, extended over a larger area by a series of squares to encompass six, eight, ten, or more compartments arranged along a central axis. Larger gardens included outer hunting areas or orchards, protected by walls or rows of cypresses or poplars.

◆ PRECEDING PAGES *The palace of Cyrus the Great at Pasargadae.* ◆ *Miniatures and carpets show the classic* chahar bagh, *divided in four by water rills meeting at a central pool. The miniature,* ABOVE, *executed in 1604 for the future Emperor Jahangir, is from the* Halnameh, *written in Herat in the 15th century. The garden, enclosed by walls and entered by a massive gateway, has sunken flowerbeds, cypresses, symbols of immortality, and spring-flowering almonds, emblems of rejuvenation in the New Year.* ◆ OPPOSITE *The Wagner garden carpet, woven in the early 17th century, has pairs of pyramidal cypresses and plane trees flanking the water rills. Waterfowl and fishes, and wild animals among the almond trees, suggest the carpet depicts a royal hunting park.*

The quadripartite layout was to be reinterpreted in Islamic terms by the Muslim Arabs after their 7th-century conquest of Persia, establishing the pattern of the celestial gardens of the sacred Koran. By the 14th century, it still presented the basic groundplan of gardens that, under Timur, were more like tented encampments, an idea carried to the northern plains of India in the early 16th century by Timur's descendant, Prince Babur, who was to become the first Mughal emperor.

In the 17th century, a basic, if somewhat derogatory, summation of the Persian garden was made by the Anglo-French jeweler, Sir John Chardin, in his *Voyages en Perse*:

> The gardens of the Persians commonly consist of one great Walk, which parts the Garden, and runs on in a straight line, border'd on each side by a row of Plantanes, with a Bason of Water in the middle of it, made proportional in Bigness to the Garden, and likewise of two other little Side-Walks, the space between them is confusedly set with Flowers, and planted with Fruit-Trees, and Rose Bushes: and these are all the decorations they have.

Garden carpets illustrate the four-fold pattern and, with Persian (and later Mughal) miniatures, confirm the basic formula. But they do more than that; they portray gardens filled with colorful flowers as well as water, trees, and fruit belying Chardin's cryptic comments. In the squares between the rills at Pasargadae, flowerbeds, sunk below the main walkways for ease of irrigation by periodic flooding, were planted with fruit trees in ordered rows, undercarpeted with spring-flowering bulbs. Architectural rigidity—

vertical walls and horizontal canals and rills—contrasted with delicate tree shapes and shadows and a pattern of flower and leaf forms. The space inside the enclosure was deliberately glorified in contrast to the hostile world without, confirming the Persians' in-built attitude toward nature in a land where habitation depends on the availability of water. As centuries passed, the Persians' love of plants was expressed in architectural decoration, in floral motifs, twining grapevines, and interlacing branches.

In a land of harsh light and with a climate too hot for exertion, shade and protection—from wind as well as sun—were essential elements of the Persian garden. Cyrus's

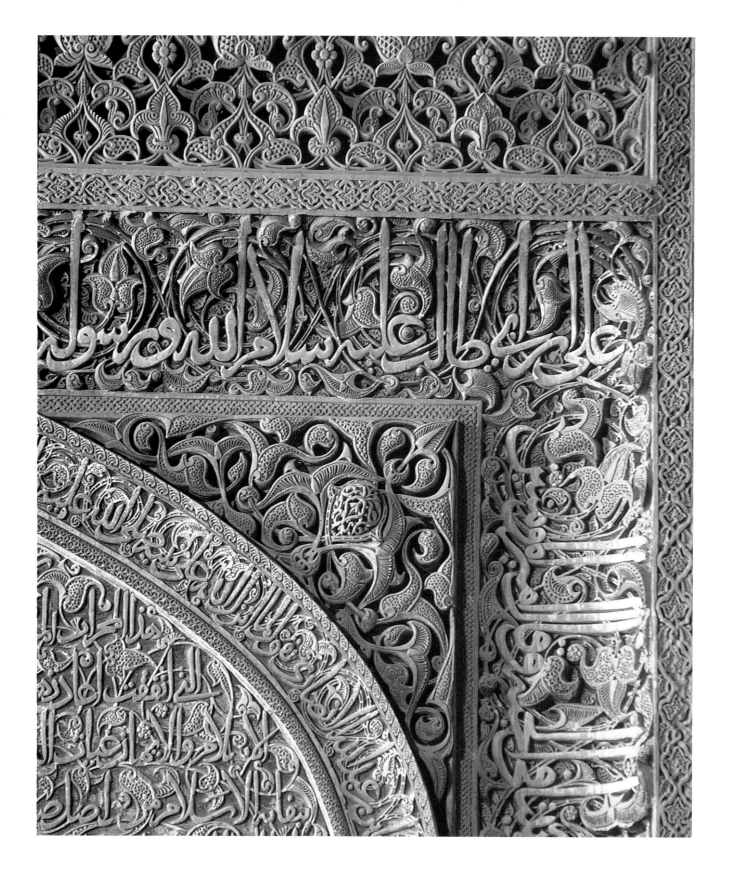

throne was set in the deep-shaded portico of the palace and his garden was probably encircled by trees in serried ranks and shaded by avenues of native cypress, eastern plane, and pine trees, watered by *jubs* (open channels). Excavations have revealed the orientation of two other open-sided pavilions from which to view the garden during the heat of the day. By the 2nd and 3rd centuries AD the deep porticoes were further developed by the Parthians into the barrel-vaulted half-spheres called *ayvans* (or *ivans*), their recessed spaces and high ceilings making a cool refuge. By Sasanian times, the towering *ayvans*, backed by deep halls, provided shady retreats overlooking substantial pools and ornamental garden layouts, often with a hunting park beyond. Under Islam, after the Arab invasion in the 7th century, the hedonistic Persian pleasure park, already regarded as a paradisiacal retreat, became the embodiment of the celestial paradise promised to a practicing Muslim.

A thousand years later, Chardin observed that gardens were for repose:

> The Persians don't walk so much in Gardens as we do, but content themselves with a bare Prospect; and breathing the fresh Air: For this End they set themselves down in some part of the Garden, at their first coming into it, and never move from their Seats till they are going out of it.

Water was an essential, but scarce resource —the element vital to life and the growth of plants in a climate that was, and still is, difficult for gardening and agriculture. Brought by underground channels and aqueducts from melting snows in the high moun-

tains, it was ordered into canals and basins, which, even in the time of Cyrus the Great, had a decorative as well as a practical function. With Islam, the channels dividing the *chahar bagh*, meeting at a central pool or pavilion, represented the four rivers of life. Over centuries, the Persians' use of

♦ *Inscriptions on the* mehrab *in the Friday Mosque in Isfahan,* OPPOSITE, *which dates to 1310, are carved in stucco on a background of flowers, leaves, and scrolls, typical of the finest Islamic work, that demonstrate the Persian reverence for nature.*
♦ *Pollarded willows,* ABOVE, *line a water course running around the perimeter of the Bagh-e Fin outside Kashan, an oasis town in the eastern foothills of the Zagros.*

water in gardens became ever more sophisticated, often in conjunction with pierced screens and other reflective surfaces to achieve a mystical symbolism. Pool shapes developed as octagons and were scalloped into lotus patterns. On sloping sites, water rippled over carved screens (later called *shadarvan* in Persia and *chadar* in India). Soothing fountains, worked by gravity, cooled the air and discouraged insects.

Pools of water mirrored the architecture of mosques, palaces, and tombs to convey a sense of openness, culminating in the effect at the Taj Mahal in India, where the canal that divides the four-fold garden reflects the entire building—doubling the apparent size of dome and minaret.

The sophisticated Achaemenid royal pleasure park appeared god-given in the arid, treeless plateau of central Iran and, even before the coming of Islam, represented paradise on earth. While it cannot be certain that Cyrus the Great subscribed to the teachings of Zoroaster, which emphasized the cultivation of the earth as a primary obligation, it is possible that the king combined Zoroastrianism, the main religion of pre-Islamic Persia, with his own mythical polytheistic beliefs. The founder of the religion, born in about 1200 BC in a pastoral area south of the Aral Sea, worshiped Ahura Mazda, the god associated with creation and fire to whom the heirs of Cyrus the Great attributed their kingship.

With Islam, gardens became places for sacred contemplation and spiritual nourishment, an interpretation of the Biblical Garden of Eden, a heritage which Islam shared with the two other great monotheist religions, Christianity and Judaism. In the Koran, this celestial paradise, in which flowers bloom and fruit ripens simultaneously, and man and beasts live in harmony and plenty, clearly refers to a garden situated in a desert comparable to those of Arabia or the Iranian plateau. In later centuries, gardens became settings for romance and pleasure and, in those created by rulers, religious meaning was overlaid by representations of power and prestige, until they resumed symbolic significance in the grand Indian tomb gardens of the 16th and 17th centuries.

• *Massive walls,* ABOVE, *thick enough to house cool pavilions, protect the Bagh-e Fin from grit-laden winds that sweep across the desert.* • *Hafez's tomb garden in Shiraz,* OPPOSITE, *is a place of pilgrimage with reflecting pools, shaded by tall palm trees, and banks of scented flowers, including annuals in terracotta pots. The 14th-century poet brought renown to his birthplace and, to this day, people seek peace in the "Garden of Paradise" surrounding the mausoleum.*

Pasargadae

Cyrus the Great's capital, built in the 6th century BC, consisted of a palace and two open-sided pavilions set in a well-watered garden. The king sat raised above his courtiers in the shade of the palace portico, its elevation emphasizing his rank. From there, he looked out onto the decorative axial limestone rills aligned with the garden's central axis.

Excavations have revealed that the main garden at Pasargadae, probably the king's private garden and by a much larger royal park, was a rectangle some 800 × 650 feet, flanked by pavilions that offered shade during the heat of the day.

In the squares between the rills, sunk below the main walkways for ease of irrigation, Cyrus will have grown fruit trees in ordered rows—pomegranates (already cultivated for centuries), wild sour cherries, and almonds —and vines and native roses, undercarpeted with clover sparkling with spring-flowering bulbs—tulips and iris—and poppies. Trees, acting as protective wind breaks and watered by *jubs*, may well have been the familiar white-stemmed poplars (probably *Populus alba* f. *pyramidalis*). Avenues of native cypress and Asian plane provided shade.

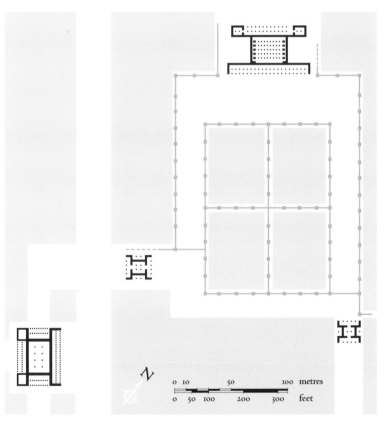

♦ *The citadel known as the Takht-e Soleiman (Throne of Solomon) stood on a vast platform,* OPPOSITE, *overlooking the site of Cyrus the Great's capital.* ♦ *Pillars and foundations,* TOP, *have enabled archaeologists to reconstruct the groundplan of the palace complex* ABOVE. ♦ *Watercourses,* LEFT, *forming the axes and dividing the garden in four, opened out at 50-foot intervals into 3-foot basins.*

2 The setting

"A savage, desolating country! But one that filled me with extraordinary elation. I have never seen anything that pleased me so well as these Persian uplands, with their enormous views, clear light, and rocky grandeur."

Vita Sackville-West *Passenger to Tehran* 1926

 THE PERSIANS HAVE ALWAYS KNOWN THEIR COUNTRY AS IRAN, AN ETHNIC NAME IMPLYING THAT it is the habitat of the Iranians, a branch of Indo-Europeans. "Iran," from the word "Aryan" meaning the "land of the nobles," was first used in about the first millennium BC. The name Persia, used by the ancient Greeks, is derived from the southwesterly province of Pars (modern Fars), which was the cradle of the Persian Empire. Here, the Achaemenids, an Iranian tribe, became the first kings of a united country. They laid out gardens at Pasargadae and Persepolis in the 6th and 5th centuries BC, and ruled over territory which stretched from the Persian Gulf to the Black Sea, from China in the east to the Mediterranean shores, and to Egypt.

Iran is a land where harsh winds and fierce dust storms sweep across the plains and water is always scarce. Few rivers and streams irrigate the Iranian plateau, most of them fading out in the heat of the desert or turning into *kavir* (salt swamp), dangerous to cross and covered with a thin glazed crust or a yellowish slime where water does not drain away. Gardens in the Western sense, with a progression of seasonal flowers, are not viable in a land with searing cold winters and burning heat in summer.

To understand how Persian gardens developed, it is important to consider the diverse topography of Iran, which is matched by extremes of climate, and to explore the growing conditions in different regions.

A BEAUTIFUL AND
EVOCATIVE COUNTRY

Iran conveys a sense of ancient, unchanging history which, in the words of Harold Nicolson, leaves the traveler "haunted by those plains of amber, those peaks of amethyst, the dignity of that crumbled magnificence, that silence of two thousand years." Away from the bustling modern cities, in spite of centuries of human depredation, the countryside remains much as he and Vita Sackville-West found it in the 1920s. "Persia has been left as it was before man's advent," she wrote.

> Here and there he had scraped a bit of the surface, and scattered a little grain; here and there, in an oasis of poplars and fruit trees outlining a stream, he had raised a village, and his black lambs skipped under the peach-blossom; but for miles there was no sign of him, nothing but the brown plains and the blue or white mountains, and the sense of space . . . I was left, breathing, with space all round me, and a serenity that looked down from the peaks on to the great bowl of the plain.

In Persia, as in most desert lands, the activities of humankind, both as cultivator and the keeper of sheep and goats, have had devastating effects on natural vegetation over the centuries, leaving only a few remnants in the remoter regions. In a country of low winter temperatures, collecting fuel for burning and for charcoal-making, as well as cutting of timber for building, has reduced the forest areas—already restricted by climate and topography—and degraded them to scrub. In many regions continuous grazing has led to the disappearance of perennial grasses and their replacement by non-palatable weeds and spiny shrubs. The cultivation of crops—and of course gardening—has also disturbed the natural vegetation.

Modern Iran covers an area of 636,000 square miles, a much smaller area than at any time in its history and, except in the narrow coastal strips, only thirty percent of the country—the central plateau—is inhabited.

Persia has always been liable to earthquakes. Every day a traveler sees evidence of damage, an example of the most serious being the 15th-century Blue Mosque at Tabriz which was destroyed by a succession of quakes. Qazvin, the province of Gilan along the Caspian shore, and Shiraz in the south have all been affected by earthquakes. Some of the earlier gardens in Shiraz that were destroyed in the early 19th century were later rebuilt by the Qajars. One of the most serious 20th-century earthquakes devastated the oasis town of Tabas, situated in the desert almost halfway between Mashad and Yazd, in 1978. The 18th-century garden, watered by rushing torrents from the mountains, miraculously survived, but the ancient mosque, windtowers. and houses were destroyed, and 25,000 people died. In 1990 48,000 people lost their lives in Gilan province.

WATER: "THE SYMBOL OF GOD'S MERCY"

On the plateau almost the only source of water is the snow which falls on the high peaks in winter and, since the 7th century BC, has been harnessed to make possible both the cultivation of fields and gardens. While water from the mountains could be diverted and stored for use in villages at their base, in open channels it quickly evaporated in the desert sun. The ancient Persians and Medes, immigrants from the Russian steppes in around 1,000 BC, who settled around the northeast of the Zagros and in the southwest on the edge of the plateau, invented an elaborate system of underground conduits to take melting snow to the orchards and fields in the dry land of the plain. Known as *qanats*, the system was brilliant in concept but highly dangerous and labor-intensive to build and maintain.

Once the water reached the point of exit, it was conducted into cisterns and into a network of *jubs* (open channels or runes), with a system of sluices for irrigating orchards, sunken flowerbeds, and avenues of trees. The distribution of water for drinking, agriculture, orchards, and gardens was strictly controlled by a powerful official, called a *mirab* (water controller, literally "prince of water.")

Cyrus the Great and his successors extended the network of *qanats* throughout the Persian Empire and, until very recent times, the ancient water ducts and flooding mechanisms met the needs of a desert existence and made the very sustenance of life possible in many rural areas of Iran. Today hydroelectric schemes in the mountains, and local reservoirs, have replaced most of the ancient conduits.

* PRECEDING PAGES *Tall poplars and spring-blossoming fruit trees grow at the base of mountains in northeast Iran, where water is provided by melting snow.* * *On the south side of the Alborz Mountains a dusting of snow in April reveals isolated clumps of junipers,* ABOVE, *which are all that remain of the original forest, destroyed over centuries by man and grazing animals.* * *A green oasis in the barren countryside,* OPPOSITE, *is watered by a mountain stream.*

The ingenious *qanat* system

Since water in open irrigation canals on the high Iranian plateau evaporates very quickly in the summer heat, the ancient Persians built a network of underground aqueducts. This was done by sinking a shaft to the permanent subterranean water level at the base of the hills; from there, a tunnel was dug to carry water to where it was needed. At intervals of 50 feet or so, further shafts were dug for removing spoil and to provide air for the underground workers. It required skill to achieve a straight line and the precise "tilt" for gravity to propel the flow of water. The excavator's guide was sometimes the shadow cast by a candle. Channels were lined with stone or tile in areas of particularly porous soil and the tunnels, dug with the simplest of tools, could run for as many as 25 miles.

Viewed from the air, the course of a *qanat* resembles a series of mounds thrown up by gigantic moles. The open hollow at the center of each mound marks a shaft to an underground conduit. The number of openings in one line may be as many as 200. Any failure of a *qanat* could lead to the death of a village, entirely dependent on the water supply for its existence. *Qanats*, in conjunction with *jubs*, fitted with sluices to allow water seepage to the roots of trees and the periodic flooding of sunken flowerbeds, made orchards and domestic gardening a possibility. *Jubs* are still evident in towns such as Isfahan and Shiraz, watering the street trees, and irrigation holes are visible in sunken beds in old gardens. Ancient *qanat* lines have been discovered all over the Middle East and on the desert route to Samarkand and into Afghanistan, the shafts sometimes proving a hazard for caravans.

The strange crater-like series of lines through the desert, visible particularly from the air, mark the *qanats*. Successive waves of Mongol invaders deliberately damaged many *qanats*—and also put sand in wells—but some survive today, although most areas receive water from modern reservoirs.

◆ *The longitudinal cross-section of a* qanat *shows how underground conduits were constructed on a slight gradient to take water from the mountains to gardens, villages, and cities. The master shaft, sunk at the foot of the mountain, was up 150 feet deep.* ◆ *Precious* qanat *water, and ice formed on frosty winter nights and collected in shallow channels, was stored in mud-brick domes, such as this,* OPPOSITE ABOVE, *near Kerman, an ancient city in southeast Iran.* ◆ *Excavated material, mounded up around an access hole,* BELOW LEFT, *marks a* qanat *shaft.* ◆ *Asian plane trees lining a street in Isfahan,* BELOW CENTER, *are still irrigated by* jubs.

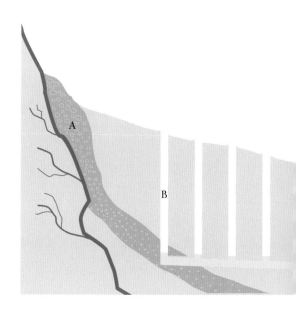

Persia is one of the highest lands in the world, and the heart of the country, "the great bowl of the plain," is a plateau, 4,000–5,000 feet in elevation and the shape of an elongated saucer. It is protected by two main mountain ranges: The Alborz that run from east to west, backing Tehran and towering above the shoreline of the Caspian Sea; and the Zagros, which cut off the plateau to the west, running parallel to the Iraq frontier and the Persian Gulf. Mountain peaks, some of which reach 15,000 feet and are snow-covered even in summer, shield the plateau from refreshing rain-bearing winds but still expose it in winter to icy air masses from Central Asia and Siberia. Annual rainfall on the central plains is 2–10 inches, almost all falling between November and April. The winters are bitter with harsh winds, followed by scorching summers and relentless sun. To the east there is desert, a vast space which extends beyond the Khorasan frontier to Afghanistan and Pakistan.

The plateau is also strewn with mountains, many running parallel from northwest to southeast to make inner closed valleys, their summits rising almost vertically, and constantly shading the tones of the buff, almost brown, landscape, with the changing light and cloud shadows. The desert traveler can always see a ring of mountains, spectacular at dawn or as the sun sets.

The plain combines steppe and desert conditions, the predominance of one or the other depending on rainfall, just as it determines the limits of cultivation, the boundary lying roughly between 10 and 12 inches of precipitation. Stands of pistachio and shrubs—such as almond and drought-resistant berberis, lonicera, and lycium—thrive on rocky hill flanks with almost treeless steppe conditions at

A shepherd and boy tend a flock of sheep and goats on the plateau below the high mountains where vegetation is sparse. Rainfall occurs mostly during winter, but a wet April will insure that the desert will "green up" before the worst of the summer heat.

rolling, flatter countryside, the scrub is composed mainly of different wormwoods, such as *Artemisia herba-alba*, dwarf bushes, grasses, and herbs which cover areas of the plateau at moderate elevation. Various thin-leaved ephedra, such as the red-flowered *E. intermedia*, are found on stony slopes and gravel terraces. Apart from the occasional cultivated orchards of pistachios and almonds and a sprinkling of short-lived annuals, there is virtually no vegetation except the camel thorn (*Acacia giraffae*, syn. *A. erioloba*), crimson-flowered in spring on bare branches. In the sun-baked *dasht* (deserts) of the plateau, only spiky bushes and prickly cushions of gray-leaved plants, which can withstand heat and lack of water, survive, although after rain in spring the desert can become "green."

The depression of the southern Sand Desert (Dasht-e Lut) has no precipitation, hence no vegetation, while the Great Salt Desert (Dasht-e Kavir), covering about 21,000 square miles, is barren because of its salinity. Attempts are being made to introduce salt-tolerant trees and shrubs (halophytes) that are naturally adapted to the environment. Many of these have no value except as fodder for sheep, goats, and camels, and as wood for fuel. In the future it may be possible to increase the salt tolerance of crops such as wheat and barley through conventional breeding and/or genetic engineering.

lower elevations, fading to a plantless landscape on the gravel-covered depressions where rainfall is less than 4 inches or where the *kavir* (saline swamps) make growth impossible. Above 6,000 feet the steppe consists of spiny bushes or brushwood of species such as *Astragaleta* and *Acantholimon*, low bushes which exude a gum substance, and occasionally gum arabic (*Acacia niloteca*), mixed with grassy and herbaceous plants including *Artemisia*. In the plains and

Today wide highways connecting the principal cities drive their way through the inner valleys, avoiding the villages, lived in by settled communities, which are located at the base of the mountains where they have always benefited from more ample water supplies. Off the main route they are hardly seen, although many cultivated orchards, enclosed

◆ ABOVE *Painted in 1431 in Herat for Shah Rokh, the miniature shows an oasis landscape in a desert setting, with fruiting palms* (Phoenix dactylifera) *and tall cypresses beside a winding stream, flanked by wild flowers. It illustrates the story of Laila, the beloved of the mad Majnun, in Nezami's* Khamseh: *Laila rests in a palm grove; Majnun, isolated and consumed with loneliness, is shown in the distance.* ◆ *Orchards, enclosed by mud and straw walls,* OPPOSITE, *are a feature of the Iranian plateau, bright with blossom in early spring and oases of green in summer.*

within umber-colored walls, mud and straw baked in the sun, are a spectacular sight: In spring a cloud of blossom, in summer a cool green to contrast with the barren beauty of the buff-colored landscape. In the remote villages, among the flat-topped houses, more walls enclose miniature orchards of pomegranates, pistachios, walnuts, and figs. In many areas, white-stemmed poplars (*Populus alba* f. *pyramidalis* from Central Asia), planted in serried ranks, mark the lines of a mountain stream or damp watercourse and edge the cultivated fields of wheat, their leaves turning golden in September before they fall. Willows, oleaster (*Elaeagnus angustifolia*), alder, and ash also reveal the presence of water.

The *garmsir* (literally "warm land") of the semitropical lowlands of the southern provinces is characterized by the cultivation of the date palm, the kunar tree (*Ziziphus spina-christi*), acacias, prosopis, and others. Date palms replace the poplars of the *sardsir* ("cold land")—the cool valleys and plateaux above regions of settled life—making green oases in the desert expanse that provide food, as well as a feast for the eye. Oleander bushes thrive in dry watercourses. The Genoese Marco Polo (*c*.1254–*c*.1324), *en route* for the East, admired the "fine groves of date-palms, which are pleasant to ride through" between Yazd and Kerman. Man has made use of the temperate climate of the province of Fars to create flourishing citrus orchards and gardens and to turn Shiraz into a poet's paradise of roses and nightingales. In the 17th century Shah 'Abbas's officials harnessed the Zayandeh Rud, the river that flows through Isfahan, to provide water for his gardens and fountains.

As well as the ruins of Pasargadae and romantic gardens in Shiraz and Isfahan, remarkable oasis gardens have survived on the central plateau. The finest are the Bagh-e Golshan in Tabas, the Bagh-e Fin outside Kashan, and the Bagh-e Shahzadeh in Mahan. Bagh-e Doulatabad in Yazd, one of the hottest places in Iran, receives water by *qanats*. The National Botanic Garden (now the Research Institute of Forests and Rangelands), created in the 1970s near Karaj west of Tehran, gets its waters from the Alborz.

Bagh-e Doulatabad

The Doulatabad Garden in Yazd, a town surrounded by desert and reputed to have hotter summers than anywhere else on the Iranian plateau, was created by Moham-mad Taqi Khan, governor of Yazd, in the second half of the 18th century. Five *qanats* were dug to bring water from Mehriz, 22 miles south of the city in the foothills of the Shirkuh Mountains. Only a quarter of the water was needed for the garden and the rest was bequeathed to the town for its use and for irrigating crops. Because of rapid evaporation, the garden had only one, octagonal, pool.

The walled garden was divided into a ceremonial reception area and a private space. A winter pavilion faced south down a long avenue flanked by pines and cypresses, and a shaded summer house, topped by a tall *badgir* (windtower), faced north. Built around an armature of wooden poles, which gives resilience to the structure, its projecting ends serving as scaffolding for maintenance, the *badgir* captures the breezes and carries them to the ground floor and underground chambers. The inward flow of air is matched by a strong updraft in the opposite side of the windtower. At Doulatabad five pools in the basement further cooled the air, reducing the temperature by at least ten degrees.

In 1888 the Persian scholar Edward G. Browne, who spent a year in Persia, found that Doulatabad was a public garden where, after wandering through the bazaars, he could rest and converse in the shade.

◆ Old grapevines and cypresses, ABOVE LEFT, *indicate the garden's former glories. ◆ Sunlight shines through open doors in the summer house,* RIGHT TOP, *beyond which lies the garden's single pool and fountain. An interior pool shivers in the breezes funneled by the* badgir, *seen from beneath,* RIGHT BELOW. *Here people sat and slept during sultry weather. ◆ Towering above the summer house, the* badgir, OPPOSITE, *is dramatically framed by dark cypresses.*

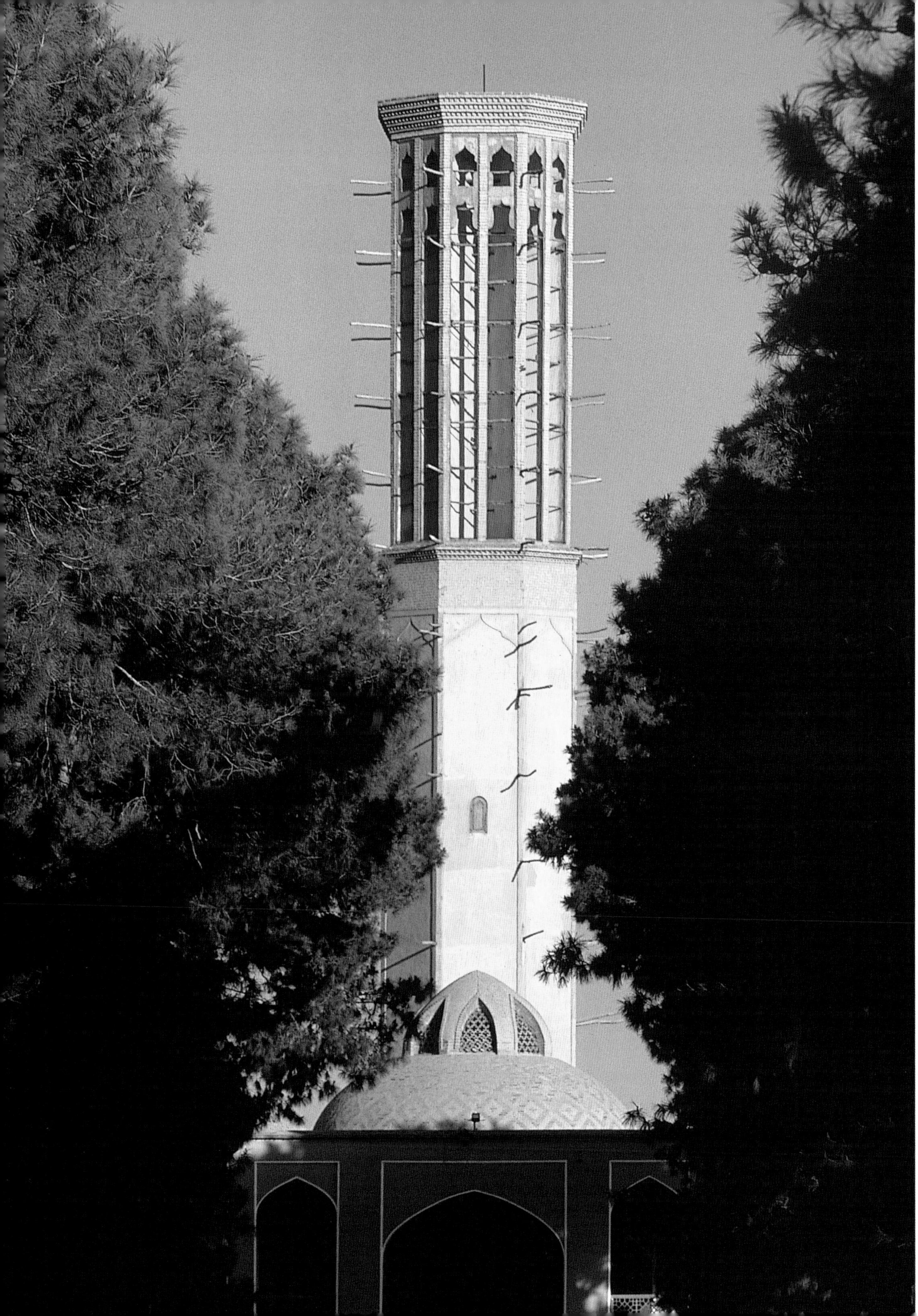

THE ALBORZ
AND THE CASPIAN

The Alborz form a great wall across the north of Iran, merging to the east with ranges running into Afghanistan and the distant Hindu Kush. In the east, between the Alborz and the Turkoman desert to the north, lies a fertile coastal plain that gives way to steppe. In the 1930s, *en route* to Mashad, Robert Byron described the contrast between the "misty Alpine blue" of the wooded mountains and the "glowing verdure" of the steppe:

> Suddenly as a ship leaves an estuary we came out on the steppe; a dazzling open sea of green. I never saw that colour before. In other greens, of emerald, jade, or malachite, the harsh deep green of the Bengal jungle, the sad cool green of Ireland, the salad green of Mediterranean vineyards, the heavy full-blown green of English summer beeches, some element of blue or yellow predominates over the others. This was a pure essence of green, indissoluble, the color of life itself.

For the traveler approaching Tehran, the view is dominated by the formerly volcanic Mount Damavand, the highest peak of the Alborz, rising 18,600 feet. Since ancient times it has been the setting for exploits of legendary heroes. Below the Alborz to the north lies Persia's only area of humid hanging forest and the descent to the lush coastal strip along the Caspian shore, 100 feet below sea level.

The Caspian or Hyrcanian forest covers 400 miles along the southern shore of the Caspian Sea, including, from east to west, part of the province of Gurgan and the provinces of Mazanderan and Gilan. Originally the forest stretched almost to the shoreline and consisted mainly of vigorous deciduous broad-leaved trees and shrubs, about fifty or sixty different species, growing in a several-storied structure. Masked at head-height by great patches of bramble, many of the trees are familiar: Linden, ash, elm (*Ulmus minor*), *Acer velutinum* (with sycamore-like leaves and upright flower panicles), hornbeam, and walnut. Less well-known trees which have their home here are ironwood (or Persian teakwood, *Parrotia persica*), *Gleditsia caspica*, *Zelkova carpinifolia*, *Albizia julibrissin*, and the oak with leaves resembling sweet chestnut (*Quercus castaneifolia*). Asian plane trees (*chenars* in Persian) and winged nut (*Pterocarya fraxinifolia*) flourish beside the riverbeds at altitudes below 1,000 feet. Pomegranates seed in freely when there is an open space.

♦ *Ironwood or Persian teakwood* (Parrotia persica), ABOVE, *is indigenous to the Caspian forest on the north side of the Alborz Mountains. With peeling bark and splendid fall coloring, this small tree or large shrub has won a place in many European gardens.* ♦ *Tea plantations,* OPPOSITE, *together with rice fields, thrive in the humidity and heat along the Caspian shore, 100 feet below sea level.*

There are also evergreen shrubs such as box (*Buxus*), cherry laurel (*Prunus laurocerasus*), butcher's broom (*Ruscus aculeatus hyrcanicus*), holly, and ferns. The lowland forest originally covered the foothills and a transitional area up to 3,000 feet, in which some cold-sensitive species cannot survive. Higher still, the montane forest is dominated by Asian or European beech until, from about 5,000 feet, beech is gradually replaced by an oak, *Quercus macranthera*, while some elm, ash, hornbeam, maple, wild pear, and juniper still survive.

Part of the forest has become grassy pasture, enclosed fields, and a remaining worthless scrub and in the lowlands it has been succeeded by terraced tea fields, rice paddies, and orange groves, which also cover areas where malarial swamps once dominated. Evaporating water from the inland sea, bounded to the west by the Caucasus and to the east and north by desert, forms clouds over its surface, which are blown south toward the mountains to give rainfall throughout the year, providing ground moisture and atmospheric humidity. The rain is heaviest on the coast and on the densely forested northern slope, with the higher mountains progressively drier.

Crossing the mountain passes of the Alborz from north to south, sometimes at a height of 7,000 feet, a traveler moves through gradual changes of vegetation—from dense woodland to open fields and onto stony desert, leaving behind the higher treeless peaks as he begins the descent through steep rocky valleys. The experience of traveling to the Caspian from Tabriz, through a road tunnel, which cuts through the mountains, is more startling. At the start of the journey there is mountainous desert with little vegetation, and then the tunnel emerges into a different world of rich green forest, with the Caspian Sea below.

Whereas atmospheric humidity prevails on the north face of the Alborz to altitudes of 5,000 feet, when forests are succeeded by *sarpagh*, the highest or alpine zone which

is beyond cultivation, the south face presents an entirely different vegetation. Here, with virtually no rainfall and exposed to the unrelenting summer sun, even before the *sarpagh* begins, the "dry" forest of juniper (*Juniperus polycarpos*, syn. *J. excelsa*), which once covered these slopes as well as both sides of the Zagros range in Khorasan, is reduced to scattered stunted specimens growing among pistachio, almond, berberis, and cotoneaster, with walnut, pomegranate, poplar, ash, willow, and tamarisk in the ravines.

Rice fields and orange groves still thrive in the rain-swept Caspian region, but few historic gardens survive. At Behshahr (formerly Ashraf) what remains of the 17th-century Chehel Sotun (Forty Columns) is now a public garden. The 20th-century Caspian Palace and its garden, created at Ramsar for the Pahlavi Shahs and set in the wooded foothills, has a well-kept French-style box parterre and some remarkable trees, including two fine Norfolk Island pines (*Araucaria heterophylla*) and a large *Pinus roxburghii*.

Gardens in the foothills of the southern Alborz include the 19th-century Cheshmeh-e 'Ali, which lies in a well-watered valley near Damghan, and the Bagh-e Mostoufi in Vanak, created in the 1930s.

Cheshmeh-e 'Ali

The gardens of Cheshmeh-e 'Ali ('Ali's Spring) lie in the foothills of the southern Alborz, northwest of Damghan. Almost certainly a pool had existed here since ancient times, bubbling from a natural spring, its volume augmented by mountain water pouring down into the western extremity of the pool in winter and spring.

During the early years of the 19th century, Fath 'Ali Shah formalized the

water, reinforcing the steep sides of the existing pool and dividing it in half by building a hunting pavilion on an island, which he used as a retreat from the summer heat of Tehran. The water garden he constructed is one of the most theatrical in Persia, although it lacks the drama of narrow cascades. The garden sits peacefully in the valley, flanked by serried ranks of the white- almost silver-stemmed poplar and overlooked by ancient plane trees, which must predate the garden making. Views to the arid southern slopes of the Alborz to the north and east confirm the contrast between the welcoming verdant oasis and nature's harsh extremes, while the vista down the valley speaks of lush meadows.

Cheshmeh-e 'Ali continued to be used as a summer retreat by the reigning shah until the end of the 19th century, but the hunting pavilion, and another building to the east backed by a stand of poplars, are now romantic ruins, turning the garden into a stage set, waiting for the actors to appear. The stream, controlled by sluice gates—a system called *ab-pakhshan*—exits at the edge of the pool and, hemmed in by poplars, ash, and willow, winds on southward to fulfil l the needs of the village and to water cultivated fields.

◆ White-stemmed poplars (Populus alba *f.* pyramidalis)*, ABOVE, planted in the serried ranks seen all over the north of Iran, provide a sheltering grove for the garden at Cheshmeh-e 'Ali, set in the mountain foothills. ◆ The ruins of Fath 'Ali Shah's open hunting pavilion, RIGHT, sit on an island in the middle of the great water tank. Within the enclosing brown walls, of bricks and baked clay, which match the buff-colored mountains outside this oasis garden, pollarded willows, a form of flowering ash* (Fraxinus ornus *f.* rotundifolia)*, and poplars are reflected in the deep pool and give welcome relief to the austerity of the encircling landscape.*

✦ *Mist rising from the valleys engulfs the mountains,* ABOVE, *that form an extension of the Zagros range and enclose the central Iranian plateau to the northwest.* ✦ *On the road between Tabriz and Qazvin, the fertile rolling plains of the lower foothills,* LEFT, *a medley of greens and wild flowers in spring, produce some of the best wheat and barley crops in Iran.* ✦ *The engraving,* OPPOSITE, *from* Voyages par la Muscovie, en Perse et aux Indes Orientales *(1718) by Cornelius de Bruyn, shows pistachio* (Pistacia atlantica), *which, as the cultivated P. vera, is an important crop on the east-facing foothills of the southern Zagros, sumach* (Rhus coriaria), Physalis alkekengi *and a fruiting almond.*

TABRIZ AND THE ZAGROS

The Zagros range, stretching 600 miles down southwest Persia in a series of ridges separated by narrow valleys, runs parallel to the Iraq frontier and the Persian Gulf. Most of the slopes are bare except for trees, mainly low-growing oak, on the wetter western slopes. The southwest face of the Zagros descends steeply to the region of Khuzestan and the delta of the Tigris and Euphrates in a series of deep ridges and valleys. On the eastern slope softer folds drop through drier foothills to the central plateau.

A semi-humid oak forest covers the outer western slopes of the Zagros, where rainfall can be 30 inches. It extends from the Turkish frontier through Iranian and Iraqi Kurdistan and Luristan into the Province of Fars. The low-growing oaks (mainly *Quercus brantii*) are widely spaced, allowing a small almond (*Prunus dulcis* formerly *Amygdalus arabicus*) with rush-like stems to flower between them, and grass and shrubby plants to grow in the light. Other trees include elm, maple, celtis, walnut, Syrian pear, and pistachio. In the damper ravines are moisture-loving poplars, willow, alder, ash (*Fraxinus ornus* f. *rotundifolia*), and plane trees. Below these slopes, leading down to the central plateau, there is an area of dry forest, requiring annual rainfall between 12 and 20 inches. Although natural vegetation is severely depleted, predominant trees are pistachio (*Pistacia atlantica*), and shrubby almond and maple (*Acer cinerascens*), besides celtis, juniper (*Juniperus polycarpos*) with other shrubs and a steppe-like groundcover. Whereas west of Tehran and Isfahan much of this dry forest has been completely destroyed, some survives in the markedly drier southeastern continuation of the Zagros and out toward the upland peaks and ranges south and east of Kerman.

In the Chahar-Mahal district west of Isfahan, and in the foothills of the Zagros to the south and west of Shiraz, are the high-altitude summer pasturelands of the Bakhtiari and the Qashqa'i, the two greatest nomad tribes of Persia. Although much reduced in number, in April the tribes, dressed in colorful clothes and the women unveiled, can still be seen herding their flocks from winter quarters on the plains to the mountains. In the mid-19th century the

Qashqa'i were considered "the most wild and barbarous of all the inhabitants of Persia" and, during the last Shah's reign, attempts were made to settle them in permanent pastures. Today policy is reversed and, to make their existence easier, they pay no taxes and arrangements are made for the peripatetic children to have teachers.

Extant gardens in northwestern Iran include Fathabad, Shah-Goli, and restored city gardens in Tabriz and the Chehel Sotun in Qazvin. In Ardabil there are remnants of the garden constructed in the early 17th century by Shah 'Abbas around the tomb of Sheikh Safi ad-Din (1252–1334), the Safavid's ancestor.

All over Iran, even in the driest, coldest zones, there is a brief but exciting explosion of innumerable bulbs, wild flowers, and blossoming trees in the spring, which comes at the vernal equinox to coincide with the celebration of *Nou Ruz* (New Year), when many Iranians sow cress or wheat seeds in terracotta pots as symbols of renewal, just as Chardin described in the 17th century:

> [The Persians] make Green Flower-Pots in the spring, which are very agreeable to the Eye; with these they adorn their Apartments, and their Gardens, by placing upon these Pots a Couch of sifted Earth, intermingled with the seed of Cresses, and keeping it always cover'd with a wet Cloth. The Rays of the Sun make the Seed sprout out, and you see the Pot all over Green, just like the Rind over-run with Moss.

◆ The nightingale perched on a rose branch, a metaphor for romance and friendship, is a frequent theme in Persian poetry. The painting, OPPOSITE, *is by Lutf 'Ali (c. 1797–1869), who originated from Shiraz, a city long associated with roses and nightingales and renowned through the centuries for its gardens. Although it is now a modern city, nightingales are still seen and heard in spring as the roses open their blooms. ◆ The pink Kashan rose,* ABOVE, *a form of* Rosa × centifolia, *has been used since ancient times to make the* golab *(rose water), which is sold today in the pavilion in the Bagh-e Fin.*

In many Persian gardens, orchards spread out laterally to the side of the main vista, and in the countryside, enclosed within brown mud walls that match the tones of the landscape and distant mountains, orchards of almonds, apricots, plums, pears, pomegranates, and wild cherries bloom in succession. Mountain bulbs and annuals with a quick growth cycle time their emergence to avoid the annual invasion of nomad herds in spring or emerge after their departure in the fall. They retreat into dormancy for the remainder of the year. Most perennials flower in the spring and shrivel up in the summer heat; a few that are unpalatable to flocks of sheep and goats stagger through, performing in the hottest months.

Roses, ranunculi, anemones, muscari, tulips, irises, and eremurus are a few of the many plants indigenous to Iran which have been translated into western gardens or are, at least, the ancestors of cultivated plants. The terms the Persians use to describe plants reveal an absorbing interest in nature, probably because of the predominance of desert areas and the shortage of water. Much of modern Persian (*Farsi*) recalls the language of ancient Sasanian Persia, although it is written in Arabic characters. Many of the words for flowers and horticulture in general have pure Persian roots. The word *gol* means both a flower and the rose, which has a major role in Persian poetry—not only are the "beloved's" physical attributes identified with the rose, but her tears are rosewater and she dwells in a rose garden (*golestan*). Indeed, *Golestan* is the title of a collection of poems and aphorisms by Sa'di, for whom roses are pieces of wisdom and clues to happiness, and the Rose Garden is wisdom itself. Understanding this imagery might have softened Vita Sackville-West's comment: "Hafez and Sadi sang frequently, even wearisomely, of roses. Yet there is no word for rose in the Persian language."

For centuries a native annual, *bostan afruz* (love-lies-bleeding, *Amaranthus caudatus*), was one of the few flowers in summer gardens, but today sunflowers, tobacco plants, salvias, and four o'clocks from South America follow

scented stocks and pansies. In Sa'di's *Bustan* of 1257, *bustan* means a simple walled orchard ("a place of scents") so that *bolbolestan* is a garden favored by a nightingale (*bolbol*). (The word *bagh*, meaning a garden, was not used until at least the 1st millennium, when the gardener became a *baghban*.)

In spite of climatic extremes, some trees are almost ubiquitous in Iran: Elm, cypress, juniper, the sycamore-like maple (*Acer velutinum*) with upright inflorescences from the Caspian, oleaster or Russian olive (*Elaeagnus angustifolia*), dwarf almond (*Prunus dulcis* formerly *Amygdalus arabicus*), and ash (*Fraxinus ornus* f. *rotundifolia*). Also widespread are exotics from other countries, such as the lavender-flowering Chinese bead tree (*Melia azedarach*) and white mulberry (*Morus alba*) for silkworm production.

Many trees are grown in gardens as structural components. Those that flank a central water channel might be Asian planes, cypresses, almonds, and elms, and by the 19th century the weeping mulberry was a popular choice for smaller gardens. Ancient cypresses, probably planted in the 1600s, line the turquoise pools at Bagh-e Fin, and cypresses and willows dominate the cascades in the 19th-century Bagh-e Shahzadeh. At the Naranjestan garden in Shiraz

♦ *Judas trees* (Cercis siliquastrum) *and scented Brompton stocks,* ABOVE, *flower profusely in the Bagh-e Eram in Shiraz, where nightingales sing.* ♦ *The gnarled cypress tree at Abarqu,* OPPOSITE, *southwest of Yazd, providing shade for lunchtime picnics, is reputed to be 4,000 years old.*

date palms flanked with orange groves mark out the central vista enclosing the flowerbeds. In Isfahan and Shiraz elms, poplars, and plane trees, their roots obtaining water from *jubs*, give welcome shade in the streets.

Elsewhere pine trees, melias, Judas trees, white mulberries, maples, and ash are used as specimens. In the northern areas, ranks of white-stemmed poplar take the place of date palms as oasis trees. The more tender poplar, *Populus euphratica*, with silver fluttering leaves, will not survive

extremes of cold but grows at Isfahan and Shiraz and thrives in the sultry desert climate of the Tabas oasis, providing a foil to dark-leaved fastigiate cypress. The importance of trees was noted by Vita Sackville-West:

> There are gardens in Persia. But they are gardens of trees, not of flowers: green wildernesses. Imagine that you have ridden in summer for four days across a plain, that you have then come to a barrier of snow-mountains and ridden up the pass; and that from the top of the pass you have seen a second barrier of mountains in the distance, a hundred miles away; that you know that beyond these mountains lies yet another plain, and another, and another; and that for days, even weeks, you must ride, with no shade, and the sun overhead, and nothing but the bleached bones of dead animals strewing the track. Then when you come to trees and running water, you will call it a garden. It will not be flowers and their garish colors that your eyes crave for, but a green cavern full of shadow.

PLANT EXPLORERS
AND TRAVELERS

Through the ages intrepid travelers have been drawn to Persia and among the first was the Genoese Marco Polo (*c*.1254–*c*.1324), who described the countryside, orchards, and gardens he saw *en route* to the East. The famous 14th-century traveler Ibn Battuta, from Tangier, came by ship to the Persian Gulf in about 1330 and thence by horse or camel into the interior, before going onto India. He praised Shiraz for its "elegant gardens and gushing streams, sumptuous bazaars and handsome thoroughfares." He noted the numerous orchards of apricots of "unrivalled quality," and quinces "unequaled for goodness of taste and size," delicious grapes and the wonderful water melons "whose like is not to be found in the world."

On his second visit to Persia, that inveterate 17th-century traveler and recorder Sir John Chardin took the hazardous route from the Black Sea, reaching Isfahan in June 1673.

• An engraving of Sir John Chardin, ABOVE, who traveled to Persia in 1664, returning to Paris in 1670 with commissions to buy jewels for Shah Soleiman II. He spent a further four years in Persia, retiring to England to avoid persecution as a Huguenot in France. In his Voyages en Perse, *Chardin provides fascinating descriptions of Persian gardens and flowers, and includes a lengthy account of the glories of Safavid Isfahan. He also records the complications of Persian court politics. • Fruiting date palms, OPPOSITE, flank the Naranjestan garden in Shiraz, towering above orange groves and providing welcome shade.*

As well as listing trees that he saw growing—willow, pine, dogwood, and the plane tree, gall-bearing oaks and resin-producing trees, almond, sweet chestnut, sallow, tamarisk, and berry-bearing bushes—he noted that aromatic herbs were common and vegetables abundant. Although often critical of Persian gardening, Chardin also describes the flowers he saw, at a time when bulbs from the Persian uplands were already familiar to Western gardeners, introduced through Constantinople as species or garden cultivars toward the end of the 16th century:

> There are all kinds of flowers in Persia that one finds in France and Europe. Fewer kinds grow in the hotter southern parts, but by the brightness of their colouring the Persian flowers are generally more beautiful than those of Europe. Along the Caspian coast there are whole forests of orange trees, single and double jasmine, all European flowers, and other species besides. At the eastern end of the coast the entire land is covered with flowers. On the western side of the plateau are found tulips, anemones, ranunculi of the finest red, and imperial crowns.

Around Isfahan, Chardin noted that "jonquils increase by themselves and there are flowers blooming all winter long."

> In season [he continues] there are seven or eight different sorts of narcissus, the lily of the valley, the lily, violets of all hues, pinks, and Spanish jasmine of a beauty and perfume surpassing anything found in Europe. There are beautiful marsh mallows, and, at Isfahan, charming short-stemmed tulips. During the winter there are white and blue hyacinths, lilies of the valley, dainty tulips, and myrrh. In spring yellow and red stock and amber seed of all colours, and a most beautiful and unusual flower called clove pink, each plant bearing some thirty flower blooms. The rose is found in five colours: white, yellow, red, Spanish rose and poppy red. Also there are "two-face" roses which

are red on one side and yellow on the other. Certain rosebushes bear yellow, yellow-white, and yellow-red roses on the same plant.

Another Frenchman, André Michaux, who was to become famous for introducing useful American trees to France, spent almost two years in Persia between 1783 and 1784. He reached Shiraz in March and traveled onto Persepolis and Isfahan and to Qazvin where the weather was salubrious, finding the wild originals of many cultivated plants, although his notes and diary give little specific plant information. From Qazvin Michaux crossed the Alborz, returning to Baghdad by 3 August, carrying with him some Persian bulbs and plants. Unfortunately, many of the "finds" proved difficult to cultivate in western Europe. Among them was the yellow prickly dwarf rose, *Rosa persica* (still often known as *Hulthemia berberidifolia*), introduced in 1789, which is not as adaptable as *Rosa foetida*, known as the

Austrian briar, introduced in the 16th century. Its double form was introduced to England in 1838 by David Wilcox.

Other plant hunters give an idea of the diversity of small flowers and bulbs to be found in the high mountains, although these need careful searching out with knowledge of different rock types and soils. In spite of seventy percent of the land being unsuitable for cultivation, more than 10,000 plant species have been recorded in Iran, their distribution in each region dependent on altitude and prevailing climatic conditions. Most are bulbous plants that need specific environmental conditions—as difficult to grow in the average Persian garden as elsewhere—and are collectors' items in specialist and botanic gardens all over the world. Some of these were noted by Isabella Bird traveling in the Zagros in May and June 1890 and by Vita Sackville-West in April 1927. Although enthusiastic amateurs (neither was a professional botanist), both had a deep interest in finding and observing the flowers of Persia. Isabella Bird described carpets of tulips, iris, primula, and blue flax. Vita Sackville-West made a twelve-day expedition from Isfahan into Bakhtiari country in spring, when many bulbs were flowering. At Gandom Kar she saw inky blue, almost black, grape hyacinths growing in great profusion "as thick in the young corn as bluebells in an English wood," crown imperials, mauve crocuses "and a small though brilliant scarlet ranunculus." She noted coarse green leaves of fall crocuses and more crown imperials "stiff as the flowers on a Gothic tapestry" growing between the boulders. There were blood-red poppies growing in a mountain cemetery. On the western slopes of the Zagros in rolling country with a rich vegetation she discovered orchises, iris, anemones, borage, convolvulus, star of Bethlehem, gladiolus,

✦ *The pomegranate* (Punica granatum), ABOVE, *is grown in gardens and orchards, surviving the heat with little water.* ✦ *The stately foxtail lily* (Eremurus olgae), OPPOSITE LEFT, *thrives in rocky semi-desert situations throughout Persia and, like the crown imperial* (Fritillaria imperialis), OPPOSITE RIGHT, *is found in the Alborz.*

and eremurus growing everywhere in great profusion, and a little scarlet tulip for which she had looked in vain in other parts of Persia.

In May and June 1960 Patrick Synge and Admiral Paul Furse traveled to and from Ankara, collecting mainly in the Alborz. Their finds included Oncocyclus irises discovered between the Azerbaijan border and Tabriz, many euphorbias, pink aethionemas, yellow onosmas and alliums, and seed of *Iris persica*, May being too late to see it in flower.

The expedition found tulips growing between 7,000 and 8,000 feet south of Tabriz, as well as muscari, puschkinias, gageas, and colchicums. Between Tabriz and Tehran the road lay over rocky semi-desert country where pale yellow holly-hocks, dwarf blue anchusas, alliums, aethionemas, mauve larkspur, and specimens of *Rosa persica* grew on the desert edge. From Tehran they ascended the Alborz by road, where the steep damper slopes yielded azure-blue ixiolirions, tulips, muscari, and various vetches, with banks of the golden rose, *Rosa foetida*, "five feet high and as much across." On north-facing slopes, they found bulbous plants in dry scree and rock, then descended through shrubby forest to a base at about 7,000 feet above the Caspian port of Chalus. There they saw red- and yellow-flowered *Tulipa montana*, *Fritillaria crassifolia* with reddish-green flowers, and a prostrate almond. More blue ixiolirions, and white and blue linums with *Geranium tuberosum* grew in the damp meadows.

In June an approach from the south to 7,000 feet below the towering Mount Damavand revealed patches of scarlet Asian poppies mingling with spikes of *Eremurus bungei* (now *E. stenophyllus* subsp. *stenophyllus*) among gray rocks, a large fennel, *Ferula rubricaulis*, with yellow umbels and stems, but fewer bulbous plants than on the western Alborz. Traveling east toward Mashad, the explorers discovered more plants on the plateau, although it was too late for flowering bulbs. On the return journey through Kurdistan, tall white hollyhocks and silvery-blue echinops were a constant feature.

In 1962 Admiral Furse and his wife spent seven months collecting in Turkey and Iran, traveling and often sleeping in a Land Rover called the "The Rose of Persia." They covered the southern Zagros in early spring and, in the plains below the west face, found wheat fields bright with red *Gladiolus segetum* (now *G. italicus*), a pink convolvulus, tall white *Ornithogalum leichtlinii*, alliums, and an ultramarine-violet teucrium. In the valleys *Tulipa systola* and tall muscari were present. South of Behbehan they found fritillaries and orchids. Crossing the ridge from Kazerun, driving through forests of *Quercus brantii*, they descended to Shiraz and proceeded past Persepolis to higher land where the yellow briar rose, *Rosa foetida*, was growing as scrub and a small anemone grew with *Iris reticulata*, its flowering already finished. Scarlet *Tulipa stapfii* was 4 inches high on the bare ridges. Returning to the southeast corner of the Zagros, they passed emerald-green cornfields and, in the watered valleys, walnuts, plum, and apricot were in bloom.

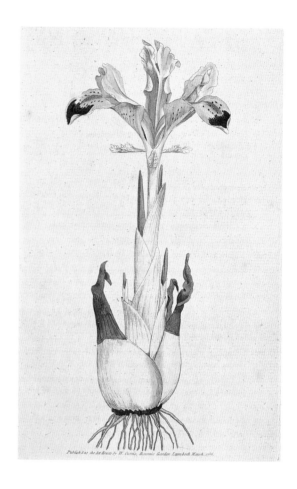

♦ *The little Persian Juno iris* (Iris persica), ABOVE, *is shown as the first plate in the* Botanical Magazine *founded by William Curtis in 1787, in which were recorded paintings of rare flowers available in contemporary nurseries. Vita Sackville-West describes finding occasional colonies of the violet-scented flowers growing on the south-facing dry mountains north of Tehran in the 1920s. Needing hot, dry summers and cold winters with snow cover, Juno irises can be cultivated only in an alpine house in temperate climates.* ♦ OPPOSITE Iris polakii, *an Oncocyclus iris, painted by Admiral Furse, who discovered it in the mountains of Iranian Kurdistan during a plant-hunting expedition with his wife to Iran and Turkey in 1962. Oncocyclus iris, needing hot, dry summers and cold, dry winters, proved to be unsuitable for cultivation in the more temperate British climate.*

MOLESKIN
BEARD

2274.

IRIS POLAKII

A

P.T. 5/65

"In front of the mountain rise the cedars in all their luxuriant abundance; their shade is pure joy. Where thorn bushes, dark gorse and fragrant plants nestle under the cedars."

Epic of Gilgamesh

WHILE THE PALACE COMPLEX AT PASARGADAE PROVIDES TANGIBLE EVIDENCE OF THE first garden layout in the West, the development of Persian gardens begins long before Cyrus the Great's victory over the Medes in 546 BC and covers an area much greater than modern Iran. Early gardens recorded in myths and literature, often confirmed by archaeological discoveries, were made in the Mesopotamian river deltas of the Euphrates and Tigris (now part of Iraq), the western foothills of the northern Zagros (today's Iranian province of Khuzestan), and in the Nile valley in Egypt. The concept of a paradise garden spread through the ancient world by military conquest and commerce: From the 2nd century BC, the main trade routes between China and the West, the Silk Road, crossed Persian lands, following the lines of oasis settlements through deserts and mountain passes.

The earliest gardens were desert oases, fenced to keep out drifting sands, as well as human and animal marauders. A natural spring provided the necessary water for life to exist, and trees gave remission from the unrelenting sun. At first purely functional, marking a division between nomadic and sedentary life, the oases dwellers developed irrigation systems and regarded the consequent vegetation and crops as direct symbols of the mercy of the gods. Luxuriant plant growth represented paradise and nature was associated with evil spirits and with death from thirst. Even in ancient times, trees, water, and earth were sacred, and wasting water was a sin. As farming skills developed, crops, fruit orchards, and gardens for pleasure flourished in more artificial situations.

THE PERFECT PLACE

Cuneiform tablets, the earliest writing known, which probably date to 4000 BC, were found in the Euphrates and Tigris valleys during 20th-century excavations and establish the concept of a paradise garden. They record how the Sumerian god of water, Enki, ordered the sun god, Utu, to create a divine garden by providing fresh water to transform the parched land of Dilmun—a land "pure, clear, and bright" whose inhabitants knew neither sickness, violence nor aging but had no fresh water—into a paradise with fruit trees, green fields, and meadows. The Sumerians, the world's first literate civilization, had descended from the foothills of northeast Mesopotamia, leaving behind forests of plane trees, scrub oak, box, cypress, and cedar, with scatterings of Judas trees, purple-flowered in spring, and poplars growing beside watercourses harnessed from melting snows. In the alluvial plains of the Euphrates and Tigris they found willows growing along the riverbanks (and date palms in the deltas) and otherwise nothing but the giant reed, *Phragmites australis*, in the swamps between the river basins.

Within a millennium the Sumerians had dug canals, drained the marshes, and harnessed the two great rivers to turn both desert and swamp into rich crop-producing land, the "fertile crescent" of the dawn of history. Periodic flooding of fields and garden beds by a system of canals controlled by sluices insured success. Within a few hundred years, their descendants had founded city states at Ur and Uruk. Cuneiform tablets of 2700 BC include fragments of the Sumerian *Epic of Gilgamesh*, which indicates that settled agricultural communities were beginning to replace a nomadic way of life: one third of Uruk is city with houses and temples, "one third is garden and one third is field."

Gilgamesh, a king of Uruk, searches out his enemy in his home on a high mountain surrounded by "luxuriant" cedars, evoking the necessity of welcome shade, and seeks the spring of eternal life in a garden:

> And lo, the gesdin [tree] shining stands
> With crystal branches in the golden sands
> In this immortal garden stands the Tree
> With trunk of gold, and beautiful to see,
> Beside a sacred fount the tree is placed.
> With emeralds and unknown gems graced.

Over centuries the valiant deeds of Gilgamesh became translated into those of other great mythical heroes—Hercules, Achilles. and Odysseus—and even into the exploits of Alexander the Great in his 4th-century sweep through the known world.

In 2250 BC, Babylon was established as the Sumerian capital. Although no plans or archaeological finds exist of garden sites before the second millennium BC, there are descriptive records of luxuriant hunting parks and of ziggurats—stepped terraces constructed to resemble mountains linking earth with heaven. One of the earliest ziggurats known to have existed was at Ur-Nammu, a Sumerian walled city to the west of the lower Euphrates, dating to between 2112 and 2095 BC. Fruit trees and vegetables were grown in the spaces between the inner and outer walls and even, perhaps, on the various levels.

From 1350 BC Assyrian kings began to create parks and gardens on the banks of the upper Tigris, irrigated by canals, and hunting parks on a grander scale in the cooler wooded foothills of the Zagros to the northeast, where the climate allowed a wider range of trees and flowers. As

♦ PRECEDING PAGES *Decorative lotus within bands of rosettes (motifs derived from Cambyses' conquest of Egypt in 524 BC) and pine trees line the ceremonial staircase of Darius I's palace at Persepolis.* ♦ *A lion and lioness from the* Bestiary of Ibn Bakhtishu, OPPOSITE, *painted in Maragheh, south of Tabriz, in 1298 during the reign of Ghazan Khan. The* Bestiary, *compiled in Baghdad in 941, was translated from Arabic into Persian by 'Abd al-Hadi. The lions in a naturalistic landscape setting of reeds—probably the native* Phragmites australis— *a fruiting tree, perhaps a pomegranate, and flowers in grass, are painted in a style showing Chinese influence brought west by invading Mongols.*

كه راه دوسَه دوزه بشركرد الخنثل ابد ناخورد وبازهاكوش برزك بيكا زفروبرد وبنه خايد
واكرنماز سودكبى خورد نيكشود وجوز رغمى خورد أزبترومانـد وددنشمانـد طلب سعدكذ وخورد

تاأزنراوبردزآيد والاتـــ اندرونى شير حمله بالآتـــ اندرونى سكماند دزاورنش وأزفرونز سبيد
ومونربتوســد وكادوانى كه ددو خروتن سبيد بنشلى كرزدكند وأزهيج جارنـكترزدكه ازنهود
وبادشاهى موتوجه برمشرنحاست كه بادشاهى شه بربيل وبركا ومبيش أزناله وبانك شترتمات

society grew more prosperous, these became areas for experimental gardening with plants (and animals) discovered on foreign campaigns, bringing a new esthetic attitude to the growing of plants for their beauty alone. Wild fruits and flowers, and herbs and spices were cultivated for pleasure as well as for use and as offerings to the gods. While retaining their "useful" role, with orchards for fruit combined with trees for shade, gardens gradually became places for recreation and amusement—pleasure gardens.

King Tiglath-pileser I (1115–1076 BC), who extended the Assyrian Empire to the Mediterranean, imported foreign trees including Kanish oak and rare fruit trees for his park at Ashur: "Cedars and box I have carried off from the countries I conquered, trees that none of my forefathers possessed, these trees I have taken and planted in my own country." Within 200 years the gardens of Ashurnasirpal II (883–859 BC) at Nimrud, with water diverted from the river through a rock-cut channel, included an even greater range of trees. As well as cedars and oaks, there were junipers, date palms, ebony (*Diospyrus ebenus*), olive, tamarisk, terebinth (*Pistacia terebinthus*), and ash, with vines, almond, pomegranate, pear, quince, fig, and apples, many collected on military campaigns as seeds or young plants.

Gardens in the Nile valley run parallel in time to developments in the fertile crescent and by the second millennium the Egyptian concept of gardening had spread to the Levant through military conquest and commerce, ultimately reaching Mesopotamia and Persia. But with very different topography and dependence on annual inundation of the Nile for irrigation, permanent planting in large parks watered by canals was impossible. Gardens in the Nile valley had to be situated on banks and terraces above the main flood valley, with protective walls holding back the ever-changing sand drifts. Water was raised by the traditional *shaduf* that is still

used in Egypt today. Elaborate Egyptian tomb paintings dating to 1500 BC depict imaginary gardens which provided sustenance for the deceased on his journey through the afterlife. There were useful fruits and vine arbors, well-stocked fishponds, and vegetation for waterfowl. Like the garden of Cyrus at Pasargadae, they included a grid system for irrigation.

The Egyptians occupied Syria and part of the Levant between *c.* 1530 and 1200 BC, bringing their own plant motifs to the east. By the 8th century BC, Egyptian plants had begun to feature as decoration in Mesopotamian art and in the gardens of other formidable Neo-Assyrian rulers: Sargon II (722–705 BC) and Sennacherib (704–681 BC). Stone reliefs from the period depict rulers banqueting in shady gardens, with trees and plants invested with symbolic meanings, such as the palm tree, associated with the gods and with royalty, and the sacred lotus (the Egyptian water lily, *Nymphaea cerulea* or *N. stellata*), which represented rebirth. There are also pine trees and cypresses (representing immortality), with lilies (almost certainly *Lilium candidum* and *L. chalcedonicum*). Edible plants are named in an early-8th-century clay tablet describing the garden of Merodach-Baladan II, a Chaldean prince who twice usurped the Babylonian throne during the reign of Sargon II, in 721 and in 703 BC.

Other edible plants were brought to Mesopotamia from northeast Turkey by Sargon II whose park at Khorasabad, northeast of Nineveh, included an artificial hill densely planted with trees, possibly cypress. His successor Sennacherib moved his court to Nineveh, where he too laid out parks, diverting mountain water by aqueduct for irrigation and planting cotton (*Gossypium herbaceum*), olive trees, and date palms, and vines in the cooler hilly regions. He used reeds (*Phragmites australis*) to help dam waters for tree

◆ *Sennacherib, the founder of Nineveh in about 700 BC, brought water from the Zagros Mountains to irrigate the parks and orchards of his new city. Nearby quarries provided blocks of stone which could be carved in bas-relief and transported to the town. Here a variety of trees, including pines, figs, and pomegranates, and vines are readily identifiable. The scallop pattern represents hilly country.*

growing: "To dam up the flow of water I made a pond and planted reeds in it … at the command of the gods, the gardens with their vines, fruit, sirdu wood and spices waxed prodigiously. The cypresses, palms, and all other trees grew magnificently and budded richly."

Sennacherib's grandson, King Ashurbanipal (668–631 BC), and his queen are depicted at Nineveh feasting under a vine arbor flanked by palms and pine trees, the head of the

◆ *A carving from the palace of Ashurbanipal, c. 645 BC, shows a paradise-garden outside Nineveh, probably created by his grandfather Sennacherib. It appears to be a "managed" landscape in which the earth has been contoured to make a park with hills and winding paths. A summer house built with columns overlooks various watercourses fed from an aqueduct.*

conquered king of the Elamites hanging from a pine tree.

Meanwhile, Esarhaddon (680–669 BC) made another great garden in Babylon, in which he tried to emulate the vegetation of the Amanus Mountains in the land of the Hittites on the Black Sea. Records of his reign describe a temple garden with fruit trees and burgeoning vegetable beds irrigated with channels of water, presumably to provide fresh produce as offerings to the gods. An earlier Babylonian text proclaims, "I planted a pure orchard for the goddess and established fruit deliveries as regular offerings."

By the end of the 7th century, the Assyrian city of Nineveh had been destroyed by a combination of Medes, Scythians, and Babylonians. The famous Hanging Gardens of Babylon, attributed to Nebuchadnezzar II (605–562 BC), grandson of the leading Babylonian conqueror, were constructed for his wife Amyitis, daughter of the King of the Medes, who in the flat plain of the river delta missed the hills and meadows of her native country to the northeast. One of the seven wonders of the ancient world, described by the Greek Diodorus 500 years later when already in decay, the gardens were composed of a series of terraces raised on vaulted brick, the upper beds irrigated by a screw system taking water from the Euphrates. The hollow shells of the brick columns were filled with soil to hold the roots of the larger trees. In this way a considerable range of exotic trees and flowers could flourish above the rooftops of the city. In recent years Saddam Hussein attempted to reconstruct the "Hanging Gardens" using modern brick.

In Persia the first region to develop a separate recorded history was Khuzestan, which bordered the fertile crescent of Mesopotamia. Here, in the 4th millennium BC, the Elamites established their own civilization, with Susa as their center, developing a script similar to the wedge-shaped cuneiform of Sumeria. Through the centuries the region was threatened and was finally devastated by the Assyrians in 650 BC. Nevertheless, the Elamite legacy was to have considerable influence on the arts of the future Persian Empire, with Elamite costume adopted as court dress. Toward the end of the second millennium BC, Aryan migrations brought tribes from Transoxiana and Turkestan, among them the Medes, who established their own territory on the high plateau in the lands east of Mesopotamia, with their capital at Ecbatana (modern Hamadan), and the Achaemenids who occupied the province of Pars further south.

The defeat of the Medes near Pasargadae in 550 BC enabled Cyrus the Great, the Achaemenid king, to establish a united kingdom which developed into a vast empire under his descendants, Cambyses II (528–522 BC) and Darius I (521–485 BC). As their empire spread to include Egypt and to touch the borders of China, the Achaemenids "borrowed" from other cultures, making use of the skills of tributary tribes in their buildings, stone reliefs, and decorations.

Cyrus restored the ancient city of the Elamites at Susa as his winter headquarters, which Darius and Artaxerxes (465–425 BC) later extended into a city of palaces and courtyards. The reigning emperor would summer at Ecbatana, ancestral capital of the Medes, 6,000 feet up in the cool air of the Zagros Mountains. The city was ringed by seven walls with terraced gardens, trees in ordered rows, and aromatic plants growing within the outer and inner fortifications. The Greek general Xenophon's *Cyropaedia*, a political romance on the life of Cyrus, written in 394 BC, makes frequent reference to the luxuriance of the royal *pairidaeza*, many of which consisted of a park large enough to include animals for the chase.

Toward the end of the 5th century BC, Darius I built a new citadel at Persepolis to replace Pasargadae as a ceremonial capital. "Royal roads," including the famous Jadeh-e Atabeg, which ran from the plains of Susiana to Persepolis, linked the cities that served as capitals of the Achaemenid kingdom. Traveling in the high ranges of Luristan in the Zagros in 1927, Vita Sackville-West came upon stretches of cobbled road that had formed part of the ancient causeway. Regions such as Bactria, Sardis in Anatolia (now western Turkey), and Memphis in Egypt were provincial centers of administration. Each region maintained its own laws and religion, with several languages and scripts recognized, and each administrator, or satrap, had a palace. In park-like gardens constructed on imperial lines, the satraps were encouraged to grow rare fruit and nut trees collected on foreign conquests. Small walled gardens within the palace complexes had underground conduits, fed by cisterns, that carried water to pools and flowerbeds. Cyrus and his successors extended the *qanat* system, allowing new gardens to be built on sites destroyed by Assyrian conquerors. The export of plants to subjugated lands was advocated: Pistachios to Aleppo, sesame to Egypt, and rice to Mesopotamia; alfalfa (*Medicago sativa*) was carried to Greece by Darius I as fodder for his horses and later to China along the Silk Road.

A hundred years after Cyrus the Great, when Lysander visited the garden of Cyrus the Younger, satrap of Sardis in Lydia from 423 to 404 BC, he described to Xenophon "the beauty of the trees, the accuracy of the spacing, the straightness of the rows, the regularity of the angles and the many thousand scents of sweet flowers which hung about them." In his *Oeconomicus* ("The Complete Householder") of 399 BC, Xenophon also noted Lysander's observation that the satrap did much of his own planning and field work, growing and transplanting seedlings. In the "'paradises' as they call them … he himself spends most of his time, except when the season precludes it." The king's attitude to husbandry, Xenophon added, ranked with the art of war as "the noblest and most necessary pursuits."

Persepolis

Persepolis, the greatest and best-preserved monument to the achievements of the Achaemenian kings, was created for the observance of *Nou Ruz* (New Year), the rebirth of nature, when the desert bursts into bloom, a spectacle which has inspired Persian art and poetry over the centuries and is still an occasion for rejoicing. Envoys from the vassal states of the Achaemenian Empire—including Elamites, Parthians, Egyptians, and Babylonians—came to Persepolis to pay tribute to their king. Led by Persians and Medes, some of whom carry flowers to indicate the arrival of spring, their static forms carved on walls and staircases still process toward the columns that supported the roof of an immense audience hall.

Repetitive stone carvings of lotus flower and leaf, cypress, palmetto, pine, and palm trees in orderly rows illustrate the Persian love of nature and the genius of craftsmanship of carving in bas-relief. The styles and motifs used in the carvings on the palace walls were determinedly eclectic, demonstrating the extent and power of the Persian Empire which encompassed the known world, with craftsmen and plants brought from all the regions.

Darius I's Tachara (Winter Palace), completed by his successor Xerxes (Ahasuerus of the Bible, 485–465), had an inner private garden with a carved water channel, overlooked by a raised platform. Below the projecting citadel lay the royal town containing Xerxes' private palace, with gardens that included an ornamental lake and a profusion of trees and flowers.

+ *Envoys from subject nations of the great Persian Empire alternate with tree motifs,* ABOVE LEFT, *on the staircase of the Apadana Palace, the great audience hall where Darius I received tributes in a ceremonial enacted at* Nou Ruz. + *The palatial complex was built on a vast artificial terrace,* ABOVE RIGHT, *some 1,476 feet long.* + *A monumental stone griffin,* OPPOSITE, *intended as a capital for the top of a column, towers over the Processional Way leading from the entrance gateway to the interior of the palace.*

ALEXANDER AND
THE HELLENIC LEGACY

The burning of Persepolis by Alexander the Great from Macedonia in 330 BC marked the final death throes of Achaemenid power and brought an inglorious end to the great Persian Empire which had dominated the world for two centuries. Four years earlier Alexander had defeated Darius III (336–333 BC) and taken possession of the palaces at Babylon, Susa. and Persepolis. He paid tribute to Cyrus the Great, a brilliant conqueror who was both powerful and merciful. In Xenophon's *Cyropaedia*, Alexander had read that his hero's tomb was surrounded by water and a garden with symmetrically arranged groves of trees, a description confirmed more than 400 years later by Arrian, Alexander's Greek biographer:

> The tomb of this Cyrus was in the territory of the Pasargadae, in the royal park; round it had been planted a grove of all sorts of trees; the grove was irrigated, and deep grass had grown in the meadow … today no water but tall willows give shade to the passing traveller.

Later Alexander was enraged to find the mausoleum had been broken into and plundered; he ordered its restoration and the entrance to be walled up.

◆ A 19th-century German map shows the route of Alexander the Great, the Achaemenid cities of Susa, Persepolis, and Ecbatana (modern Hamadan), and the extent of Alexander's Empire at the time of his death at Babylon in 323 BC. The Achaemenid Empire (558–331 BC) was almost as extensive, failing only to encompass the Athenian Greek mainland, the eastern provinces of the Hindu Kush, and lands across the Indus River in India. Alexander's conquest marked a turning point in the history and culture of the vast region, beginning a period of hellenization under the Seleucid dynasty that persisted for more than a century, in spite of increasing incursions by the Parthians.

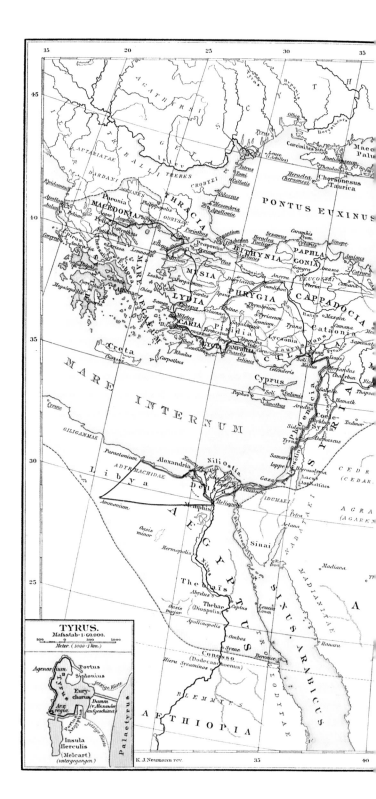

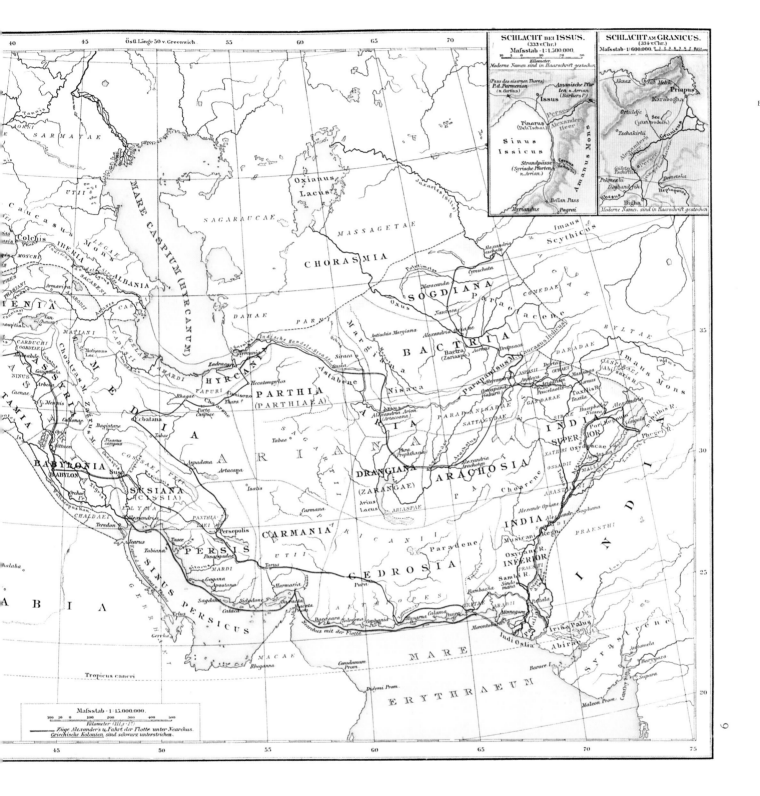

SCHLACHT bei ISSUS.
(333 v.Chr.)
Maſsstab · 1:1.500.000.
Kilometer.
Moderne Namen sind in Haarschrift gestochen.

SCHLACHT am GRANICUS.
(334 v.Chr.)
Maſsstab · 1:600.000.
Moderne Namen sind in Haarschrift gestochen.

Maſsstab · 1:15.000.000.
Kilometer (111,1·1°)
Züge Alexander's u. Fahrt der Flotte unter Nearchus.
Griechische Kolonien sind schwarz unterstrichen.

On his return to Persia from India, Alexander made Ecbatana his headquarters, but his sojourn there was short-lived and he died at Babylon in 323 BC. The lands he had conquered were divided, and were to remain so until the Arab conquest in AD 637, ruled for more than a century by Alexander's generals, the Greek-influenced Seleucids, and their descendants. They expanded agricultural development, introducing triple rotation of crops, a new plow, and cultivated improved fruiting vines; cotton, the citron, melons, sesame seed, dates, and figs traveled from Persia as far as Italy. The Greeks were taken with the wild saffron, *Crocus sativus*, growing in eastern Iran, already a valuable commercial crop for the Persians and forgotten by Greece since Minoan times when it was grown on the island of Santorini.

Alexander's generals inherited the well-maintained network of roads which had bound the vast empire together and, as they journeyed east, discovered the far-flung oases in which groves of trees were laid out in formal order with aromatic shrubs and well-watered gardens. Plants from as far

afield as India traveled back to Greece, to be examined and categorized by Aristotle and his pupil Theophrastus (*c.* 370–*c.* 286 BC) in Athens, the latter's *An Enquiry into Plants* being a systematic classification of known plants, the first in Western literature, and a description of their medicinal uses. Theophrastus included cotton (*Gossypium herbaceum*), which had been introduced by Sennacherib to Khorasabad on the upper Tigris in 700 BC, the banyan tree (*Ficus benghalensis*), described by Alexander's admiral Nearchus growing on the northern plains of India, mangroves from the Persian Gulf, and spiny euphorbias from Baluchistan. In Alexandria and in the Greek colonies of Asia Minor and Sicily, and later in Roman Italy, luxurious parks and gardens were laid out in emulation of Persian schemes.

The Seleucids kept Alexander's Hellenic legacy alight for more than a century, although the fragmented empire was threatened by separatist tendencies in the regions and by Roman territorial ambitions. By the first centuries AD the Parthians, who came from a province to the northeast of Persia between Media and Bactria, pushed the Hellenistic Seleucids further west and reunified much of the original Persian Empire, absorbing much of Hellenic culture while maintaining their tribal distinctions. Although closely allied to the neighboring Iranians in race and language, the Parthians left the people of Fars to retain their Achaemenid traditions, while acknowledging the suzerainty of their neighbors.

Basically nomads, the Parthians built substantial terraced palaces surrounded by gardens and parks. By 138 BC they had made their capital at Ctesiphon on the east bank of the River Tigris. Their major contribution to architecture was the *ayvan*. The deep, vaulted hall, enclosed on three sides, but with the third

• The tomb of Cyrus the Great at Pasargadae, ABOVE, *in an engraving from Flandin and Coste's* Voyages en Perse *1840–1842. • The tomb,* OPPOSITE, *once lay in a garden where groves of trees grew in a lush meadow. The base of the tomb, built with stones cut square and raised into rectangular form, was capped by a gabled roof. Cyrus died in battle in 528 BC. He was laid in a golden sarcophagus in the tomb's inner chamber where an inscription read: "Grudge me not this little earth that covereth my body."*

open as a gigantic arch, provided a cool retreat from which to view a courtyard or garden. The Parthians also introduced stucco, a plaster to strengthen mud-brick walls, which could be carved or moulded into ornamental forms to define the buildings contained in the gardens or looking out over them—a preparation for the exquisite floral and geometric decorations deriving from arabesques developed by both the Umayyad dynasty in Syria and Spain and later by the 'Abbasids elsewhere in the Middle East.

According to records, it was under the Parthians that peaches, apricots, and silk—on the first occasion in exchange for an ostrich egg and some conjurers—came to Persia,

brought on the trans-Asian highway from distant China, later known as the Silk Road. It was to be many more centuries before the silk worm was smuggled out of China to make possible the home manufacture of precious silk for the bazaars of Constantinople and Persia.

The Parthians provided the only effective opposition to the Roman generals invading their empire and wars persisted throughout their rule from 223 BC to AD 226. Exotic *paradeisos* glimpsed on their military campaigns inspired the Romans returning to Italy to lay out great villa gardens near Rome and in the provinces from the 2nd century BC. In 62 BC the Roman general Lucullus returned to his own city

♦ *The crowning of Ardeshir I,* ABOVE, *founder of the Sasanian dynasty, is carved in the same rock face as the tombs of Darius I and three of his successors at Naqsh-e Rostam, near Persepolis. Ahura Mazda, the Zoroastrian god, invests Ardeshir with a beribboned crown.* ♦ *The engraving,* RIGHT, *from Flandin and Coste's* Voyages en Perse 1840–1842, *is of the Sasanid palace of Firuzabad, built outside the walls of Ardeshir's circular city of Gur, which was the prototype for 'Abbasid Baghdad. The monumental* ayvan *and the spring-fed pool are now all that remain of the palace and elaborate garden.*

with peaches (originally from China), apricots, and cherry trees, the first in Europe, to decorate his grand Persian-style garden, situated on the Pincian Hill above the Spanish Steps.

DYNASTIC GARDENS

Monumental rock-cut panels, glorifying victorious kings and showing their vanquished foes—including Roman emperors—remain throughout south and eastern Iran to proclaim the power and glory of the Sasanian Empire which was established in AD 226. When Ardeshir I (who reigned 226–240), a Persian vassal king who claimed descent from the Achaemenids, defeated the last king of the Parthians,

he assumed the title *Shahanshah*, or "King of Kings." The Sasanian empire, almost as grand as that of the Achaemenids and effectively dividing the civilized western world between Persia and Rome, was renowned for its riches and for the building of monumental palaces and gardens from the Euphrates to Afghanistan.

Ardeshir's palace at Firuzabad, south of Shiraz in Fars, where water from a natural spring was diverted into channels for an elaborate enclosed garden, is what Robert Byron describes in *The Road to Oxiana* as a "landmark in the development of building." The Parthian *ayvan* has become both grander and airier and, wrote Byron, "One can see that a

barrel vaulted room is gone, but two of the transverse walls whose semicircular walls supported it still stand beside the dome chambers … Its revelation is the squinch, a simple arch across the angle of the two walls." By distributing the weight, the squinch allowed the walls to support a dome. "Henceforth," adds Byron, "as squinches were multiplied into zones of stalactites and bats'-wings, a dome became possible to buildings of all shapes and sizes." Today, the vault of the central *ayvan*, spanning 42 feet, fronts the remains of a huge *talar* (hall) towering above a spring-fed circular pool, which is all that remains of the garden. Red roses, cultivated for *'atr* (rose essence) for export to China, India, and Egypt, grew on the plain of Firuzabad.

Shapur I (242–71) built royal palaces at Bishapur southwest of Shiraz and at the Taq-i Kesra at Ctesiphon. Partially destroyed by the conquering Arabs in 642, the vast remaining *ayvan* of the palace at Taq-i Kesra is the earliest evidence of a building in a royal Sasanian garden. It is 85 feet high, spans 72 feet—wider than any vault in Europe—and the hall is 145 feet deep. By the time of Khosrou I in the 6th century, the famous "Spring of Khosrou" (Khusraw Nushirvan—known in the west as Chosroes) carpet lay on a marble pavement in the great vaulted audience hall. Modeled on a royal garden and measuring 85 × 36 feet, the carpet was woven in heavy silk. Tenth-century Persian historians elaborated on its appearance. The design, as in a real garden, was divided into flowerbeds and water channels which intersect at pavilions. Royal craftsmen had used golden threads to represent earth, shimmering crystal for water in the channels, and pearls for the gravel paths. Fruit trees in the geometric plots had trunks and branches shaped in silver and gold, with precious stones representing flowers and fruit. Many of the garden features outlined in the descriptions of the carpet have been confirmed by

♦ *Part of the façade and the* ayvan *of the great audience hall, where the "Spring of Khosrou" carpet was displayed, are all that remain of the Sasanian Palace of Ctesiphon at Taq-i Kesra on the Tigris,* OPPOSITE. ♦ *The engraving by Pascal Coste,* ABOVE, *shows the vast parabolic arches, constructed without scaffolding—an impressive feat in a relatively treeless region. Deep, vaulted halls, open at one end and overlooking a courtyard or garden, were invented by the Parthians and taken to new heights by the Sasanians.*

excavations at Emarat-i Khosrou, one of the 7th-century gardens in Kermanshah, built by Khosrou II Parviz (591–628) for his Armenian queen, Shirin. A great pool lay behind the monumental entrance portal set in the east side of the enclosing wall of a 300-acre pleasure park which, according to the 13th-century Arab historian Yaqut, was "one of the wonders of the world."

The Sasanians also re-established Zoroastrianism as the official state religion, thus linking their dynasty to Cyrus the Great, Darius I, and the past glories of the Achaemenids. Throughout their lands they built temples where the eternal fire was guarded and open-air altars for the worship of Ahura Mazda. After AD 224 the Sasanians revived the cult, calling it Mazdaism, and compiled a religious scripture, the *Avesta*, taken from the ancient hymns, the *Gathas* of Zoroaster.

Shapur II (310–79) created a vast walled park in the mountains of Azerbaijan in northwest Persia as a sanctuary for the water goddess Anahita. This sacred mountain top, its exact location remaining unidentified for centuries, represented a point of contact between heaven and earth, and is now identified as the holy city of Shiz, which was probably a Zoroastrian site even in Achaemenid times. Today it is called the Takht-e Soleiman (Throne of Solomon). Later the site was further enriched with more ceremonial buildings but the high vaulted *ayvan*, built in 618 by Khosrou II, was destroyed by the Byzantine Emperor Heraclius in 628.

Khosrou II, conqueror of Jerusalem but one of the last and least competent of the royal line, is best remembered

This garden carpet, woven in the 17th century, echoes descriptions of the famous 6th-century "Spring of Khosrou" carpet, which was assembled on a pattern similar to that of the palace garden of Cyrus the Great at Pasargadae of a thousand years earlier. Here water rills meet at a central pavilion to form the chahar bagh *layout.*

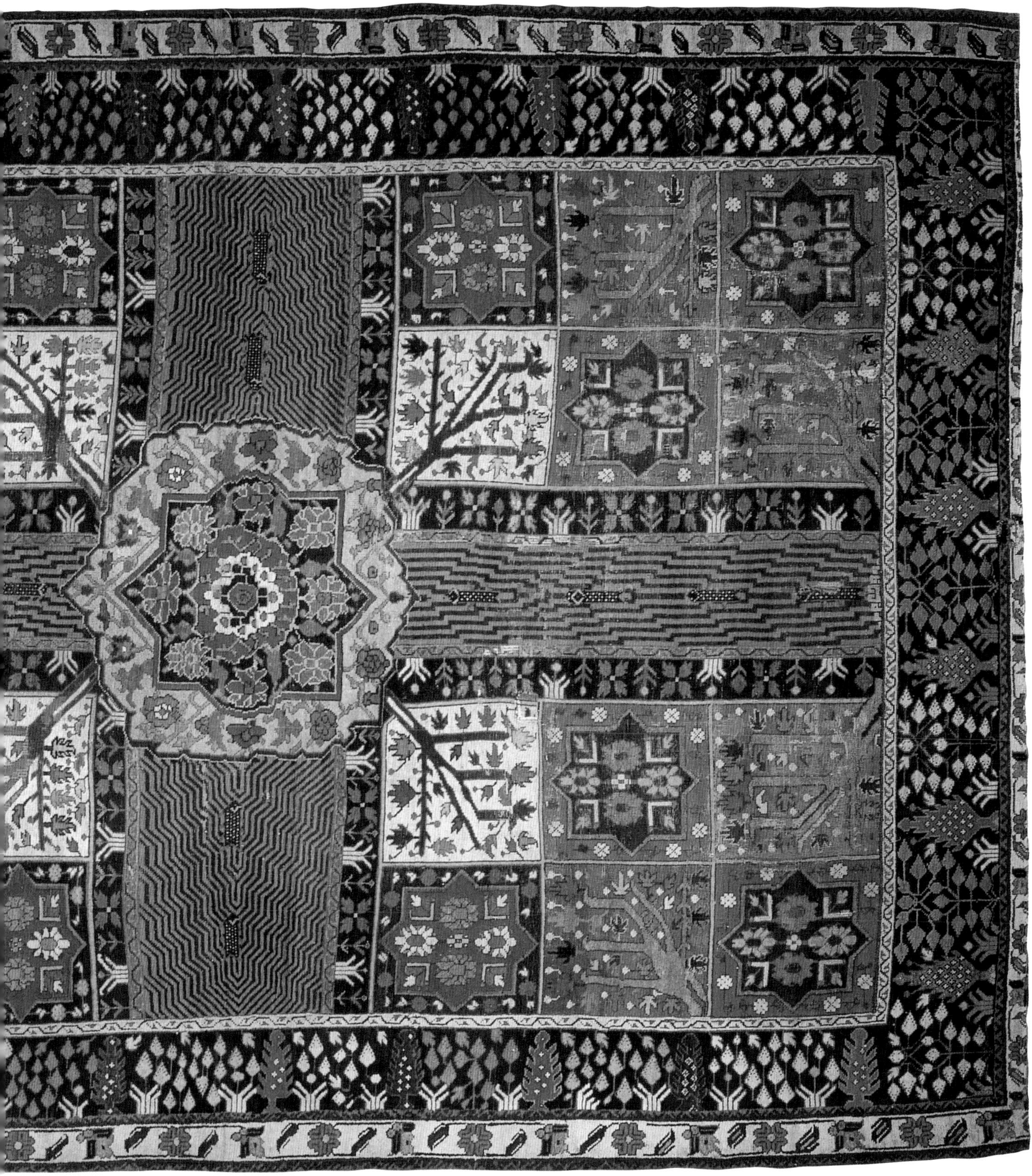

for his amours related in a romance written by Nezami in the 12th century. He made other gardens as retreats for Shirin in the western foothills of the Zagros. Near Emarat-i Khosrou at Qasr-e Shirin, and also constructed on a high terrace above vaulted chambers, was the smaller palace now known as Haush Kuri (also as Haush Khaneh). The Taq-e Bostan near Kermanshah was on a dramatic cliff site, with concealed grottoes formed into massive *ayvans*. A crystalline spring gushed out of the rocks to feed a wide pool, and carvings depicted a tree of life and hunting scenes.

For modern Iranians, the larger-than-life Sasanian Empire retains an aura of glory. It not only lasted longer than any other purely Iranian dynasty, but also appears to have a more abstract value based on what is called *Iranshahr*, a concept covering not just the land where Iranians lived and the religion of Zoroaster held sway, but also something greater—the lands ruled over by the "King of Kings." Over a period of 400 years the Sasanian kings built massive palaces and carved gigantic bas-reliefs that glorified the monarchy. They established a centralized bureaucratic empire and maintained a court of fabled splendor and majesty. Courtiers were not allowed within 30 feet of the king on ceremonial occasions and an approaching subject had to tie a handkerchief over his nose and mouth so as not to pollute the royal presence.

Sasanian literature included texts outlining court practice and learned works—especially on the subject of medicine. Many books were translated from Greek, Sanskrit, and Syriac. Folk tales and unwritten stories for the less educated were to be resurrected in later epics such as Ferdousi's *Shahnameh*, which evokes the palace gardens of the Sasanian era, and Nezami's *Khamseh*.

After the death of Khosrou in 628, political unity collapsed and the Sasanian Empire was easily overwhelmed when the Arab army launched its first attacks in 633, a year after the death of Mohammad in Mecca when the direction of the Islamic world was handed over to the caliphs (*khalifa* meaning successor or deputy).

◆ *The 19th-century engraving,* ABOVE, *shows the grottoes in the cliff that form shady* ayvans *at the Taq-e Bostan, Khosrou II's paradise garden at the foot of the mountains near Kermanshah (Bakhtaran). Water springing from the huge cliff face fed a pool, the garden projecting into the landscape. Magnificent low-relief floral carving decorating the entrance includes hunting scenes and a tree of life.* ◆ *Khosrou's first view of the beautiful Shirin,* OPPOSITE, *brushing her hair after bathing in a stream, is set in a strange landscape, with unrealistic rocks, the artist relying on a pictorial repertory for flowers, clouds, trees and figures. The miniature was painted in Shiraz in 1584.*

4   A spiritual dimension

"These gardens make us long ardently for Paradise and thus we eschew more sins and shun evil deeds." al-Bohtori

 WHEN MOHAMMAD'S MUSLIM FOLLOWERS SWEPT INTO MESO-POTAMIA AND PERSIA IN THE 7th century the Sasanian lands they conquered included the regions of ancient Sumeria, Babylon, and Assyria and stretched as far east as Kabul. The Arabs inherited an empire with a flourishing garden tradition that had existed for more than a thousand years, a tradition that encompassed enclosed gardens recalling the biblical Garden of Eden and vast royal gardens overshadowed by towering *ayvans* that were to form the prototype of Islamic mosques. The invaders found gardens that channeled water from rivers and, on the Persian plateau, desert *pairidaeza* fed by *qanat*. They discovered, too, a wealth of unfamiliar plants growing in the fertile valleys and mountain foothills. When Ctesiphon, the Sasanian capital, fell in AD 637, the conquerors came upon the palace at Taq-i Kesra, decorated with great refinement and with exquisite carpets on the floors.

The Arabs brought a new alphabet, to be adopted in the vanquished empire, and a new religion that revolutionized its culture. Architecture, painting, calligraphy, and gardens—all had symbolic meaning to inspire the righteous with beauty. Both the hedonistic Persian pleasure park and the paradisiacal retreat acquired a new spiritual dimension, interpretations taken from the Koran. Within a hundred years, Islam and the concept of the enclosed garden as the earthly embodiment of the celestial paradise had spread throughout the Middle East and to Egypt, North Africa, and Spain, and by the 16th century to Mughal India. For the next thousand years the Koranic Paradise was the basis on which gardens were created in the Islamic world.

THE KORANIC PARADISE

The Koran, revealed to Mohammad verse by verse in Mecca early in the 7th century, gave his caliphs a mission—to create a just community in which all members were treated with respect—and offered the Muslim faithful a code for life that culminated in paradise "abounding in branches, therein fountains of running water, and of every fruit there shall be two kinds." The believers shall find themselves "reclining upon couches lined with brocade, the fruits of the garden nigh to gather; and will find therein maidens restraining their glances ... lovely as rubies, beautiful as coral" (Sura 55: 48–76). Gardens were part of the interpretation of a faith that filled the whole of life of a believer (Sura 47: 15ff):

This is the similitude of Paradise
which the god-fearing have been promised:
therein are rivers of water unstaling,
rivers of milk unchanging in flavour,
and rivers of wine—a delight
to the drinkers,
rivers, too, of honey purified,
and therein for them is every fruit
and forgiveness from their Lord.

As Mohammad was considered the last of the Biblical prophets, the celestial garden, known as *jannat*, is a Muslim interpretation of the Garden of Eden, already described in Genesis. However, the Koranic revelations are more specific about the layout, which is clearly inspired by the need for refreshment in arid surroundings. The lands over which Islam prevailed during the first centuries were desert countries that depended on the concept of the "watered oasis." There are four-walled gardens in Paradise, divided in two pairs with symbolic fruits, the fig and pomegranate, the olive and date palm, in each, with intersecting walkways lining water channels representing the four rivers of life—of water,

milk, wine, and honey. Besides four fruits there are four fountains, in the lower garden "two fountains of running water" and in the higher "green, green pastures ... two fountains of gushing water." (Sura 55: 50–76).

The basic quadripartite geometry of the *pairidaeza* that had evolved from the necessities of irrigation was given new meaning under Islam. For the Muslim the number four had cosmic significance, whereby the cube representing nature's manifestations interacted with the heaven-inspired dynamic circle to dictate the development of all sacred architecture. The square within a circle (or circle within a square) became an octagon, the principle shape developed in architecture by the squinch which made it possible to place a circular dome over a square building. The four-fold garden was an open-air expression of the theme that could be interpreted inside a courtyard enclosure for private or royal use or extended to incorporate outer areas of orchards, protected by rows of cypresses or poplars if not by high walls. The place of refuge from the harsh desert became an expression of spiritual understanding.

There are more than one hundred references to the paradise garden in the Koran, and the phrase most often used is "Gardens underneath which Rivers flow," which probably referred to the immemorial *qanat* system. On a more spiritual level the "waters flowing underneath" suggest the nourishment of the "garden within," the garden of the heart, by the everflowing waters of the spirit which serve to purify the soul of the faithful on the journey through life.

The Arabs found the ancient *qanat* system on the Persian plateau and irrigation canals in the deltas of the Tigris and Euphrates. As in the early oasis gardens, water—still and reflecting in pools, forever running in intersecting channels—was the symbol of God's mercy, and wasting it was forbidden. A centrally placed ablution pool in the inner courtyards of mosques symbolized the oasis surrounded by

◆ PRECEDING PAGES *Pomegranate and walnut trees shade a courtyard in the Imam Mosque in Isfahan, a teaching area where students recite the Koran.* ◆ *A reflecting pool in the shrine of Ne'matollah Vali at Mahan,* OPPOSITE, *symbolizes the longed-for oasis in the desert.*

♦ *The Barada Mosaics,* ABOVE, *in the ambulatory of the Great Mosque at Damascus, built by the Umayyads on the site of a Byzantine basilica between 706 and 715, show a series of plant and tree motifs above the columns, demonstrating an early interest in the landscape. The monumental trees depicted are arranged in groves, sheltering buildings beside a river. The mosaics are named for the River Barada which flows through the city of Damascus.* ♦ *The Imam Mosque courtyard in Isfahan,* OPPOSITE. *Water, essential for ablutions before prayer, cools the air and, as an emblem of survival in a desert country, refreshes the soul.*

desert and, by reflecting the main dome and *ayvan*, also doubled their importance, increasing the feeling of space. The pool, the means of purification before prayer, became as essential as the carved *mehrab* inside the mosque that showed the direction of Mecca. The vast courtyard of the 8th-century Great Mosque in Damascus evoked wide expanses of desert around its central ablution pool. The courtyard arches were decorated with mosaics depicting trees and water to celebrate the idea of landscape.

We know from the Koran that fruit trees would provide both shade and sustenance in the gardens of Paradise, with water to cool the air and flowers giving scent and color. The terrestrial Persian garden described in Persian poetry and portrayed in miniature paintings combined the Koranic ideal with a more practical approach representing real gardens. Miniatures showed buildings set in gardens enclosed by high walls and outer landscapes with wild flowers growing beside streams and on hillsides. Beds where fruit trees gave dappled shade to spring-flowering bulbs and clovers were set below the intersecting walkways lining narrow water channels to allow periodic flooding. Plane trees, cypresses, and poplars (or date palms in a favorable climate) provided shade and protection from wind. Any green site became sacred and trees acquired symbolic meanings: plane trees were associated with life-giving water, the evergreen cypress represented immortality, and the flowering almond the regeneration of the earth in springtime, while the date palm provided all-year-round sustenance.

As the centuries passed, the desert dweller's love and appreciation of nature's bounties came to be reflected in the decoration of buildings and gateways of mosques and gardens. Floral motifs and abstract and geometric patterns derived from the twining branches of vines linked religion with the idea of growth, abundance, and fertility.

After Mohammad's death, the Arabs took their new faith to the richer settled lands beyond the Arabian peninsula. Arab warriors cut up the "Spring of Khosrou" carpet that lay on the marble pavement in the vast audience hall at Taq-i Kesra (Ctesiphon), and divided it as booty. From the beginning, and unlike many conquering armies, the Muslims appreciated the sophistication of the empire they inherited and showed restraint in imposing their religion. Adhering to the revelations to Mohammad in the Koran that emphasize man's duty to preserve and protect nature, which has a divine source, they taught respect for the lands they acquired. The first Umayyad caliph, Abu Bakr, who reigned from Damascus (632–4), ordered his soldiers to refrain from burning cornfields or cutting down orchards and palm trees.

The Arabs, unskilled in running an empire, were readily influenced by Persian efficiency and culture. The Persians, many converting from Zoroastrianism to Islam, became powerful in the administration of the new empire, besides introducing the Arabs to new heights of luxury and sophistication. While gardens developed a sacred interpretation, Muslim rulers also made pleasure parks, continuing the Achaemenid and Sasanian practice of creating gardens in

the environs of royal palaces and pavilions. The ancient tradition of the watered "oasis" lived on and shaped the court life of Muslim rulers in Baghdad, Persia, and other desert countries where Islam prevailed.

The lands conquered by Islam were ruled by the Umayyad dynasty in Damascus until 750, when power transferred to the 'Abbasids. In 762–3 the first 'Abbasid caliph, al-Mansur, built his new capital Baghdad on the west bank of the Tigris near the former Sasanian capital at Ctesiphon. Excavations of Baghdad, a city built over many times in successive centuries, have failed to reveal the foundations of any gardens from the 'Abbasid era, but contemporary visitors wrote about its layout and left useful if somewhat fanciful accounts of luxurious gardens. The city was circular in plan, possibly inspired by Ardeshir's Sasanian capital at Firuzabad or even the Zoroastrian city of Shiz in the northwestern mountains, its architectural schemes, derived from those of the Persians, superseding styles of the earlier Byzantine-influenced Umayyad emanating from Syria. The royal palace was a self-sufficient complex, the city's focal point, reflecting the ruler's claim to the highest place, almost next to God. Within the encircling wall there were both public gardens and inner and private courtyard gardens with pools and fountains for the ruler, and his wives and children. Offices, reception rooms, a bathhouse, and, of course, gardens radiated from the center for as much as a mile on the principal axis and half a mile along secondary axes.

The 'Abbasid caliphs surrounded themselves with guards and court protocol to preserve their aloofness, using belvederes to view the city, which were later adopted by the Moors in Andalusia as miradors framing views of garden or landscape. Palaces on the riverbank, set in fantastic gardens resembling those of the Koranic Paradise where the caliph could be seen, at a distance, by the populace, added to the illusion of his god-like status.

However, the topography of lower Mesopotamia (more or less modern Iraq) differs greatly from the arid Persian plateau and the hilly country to the north, and Persian traditions were not the only influence on the emerging 'Abbasid garden culture. Under the liberal-minded and religiously tolerant caliphs, Baghdad became a cultural mix where Christians, Jews, and Turks, as well as Persians, contributed to the organization of the capital and played a part in how future gardens developed. For centuries the Nestorian Christians, a dissident offshoot from Constantinople, had been making gardens around monasteries in the delta, stamping them with a joy in nature very different from the Sasanian expressions of power and prestige. The delightful garden of the monastery of Mar Yunan, not far from the first 'Abbasid capital, was described by as-Shaboshti, a contemporary poet:

> Like a lover's eyes watching his beloved so the narcissus are,
>   without fear or caution
> And when the red anemones appear in full bloom
>   glowing like fiery flames
> Or like a vast red carpet unrolling in honour of
>   a mighty king
> And the tender violet in the garden resembles a pinch
>   brought on a virgin's cheeks
> Daisy, lily of the valley beautifully blossoming together
>   with ox-eyes and wormwood gloriously brilliant.

Baghdad absorbed a vast number of Christian monasteries and some mosques were established in existing gardens. Al-Mansur's own garden was built in the monastery of Mar Fathion, a site chosen for its delightful position on the banks of the Tigris.

While monastic styles at first influenced the 'Abbasids, restraint was gradually overlaid with Persian extravagance, described in contemporary accounts that conjure the fabulous tales in *The Thousand and One Nights*, written during the reign of the Caliph Harun ar-Rashid (786–809). "The new kiosk is a palace in the midst of two gardens," wrote two ambassadors sent to Baghdad by the Byzantine Emperor of Constantinople in 917.

In the center was an artificial pond, round which flows a stream in a conduit … that is more lustrous than polished silver. This pond was thirty cubits in length by twenty across and round it was set four magnificent pavilions with gilt seats adorned with embroidery … all around extended a garden with lawns and palm trees … their number was four hundred and the height of each five cubits … All these palms bore full-grown dates … ever ripe and did not decay.

The ambassadors' account of the palace gardens on the east banks of the Tigris, twenty-three in all, included that of the House of the Tree, a garden reached through a vast menagerie. The tree, standing in the center of a great pond in front of a large reception room, had eighteen boughs of gold and silver covered with all sorts of fruit made of precious stones. Elsewhere, in a Roman-style hippodrome, mechanical silver birds, worked by hydraulic devices of the sort studied in Alexandria in Hellenistic times, perched on golden trees and sang and whistled as the breezes passed through. The caliph showed the ambassadors a lake of tin more resplendent than polished silver, "measuring 30 by 20 metres" with four pleasure boats covered with gold-embroidered Egyptian linen. Another more sober-minded 'Abbasid ruler grew orange trees from Basra and rare trees from Oman and India in his garden, 1,640 yards square, where "fruits gleamed yellow

◆ *Part of a door from a 9th-century palace in Samarra, north of Baghdad, preserved under sand drifts until discovered by archaeologists in the 20th century.*

and red, bright as the stars of heaven in a dusky night."

The establishment of the new city of Baghdad ushered in a period of intense intellectual activity. The city attracted Greek, Syrian, Egyptian, and Latin scholars, besides the medley of races already in the region. Its fame for the pursuit and dissemination of knowledge continued through the next centuries, while Cordoba in Andalusia became the scholarly center of Europe. Greek and Latin texts on medicine and plants that were translated into Arabic included Dioscorides' 1st-century herbal, *De Materia Medica*, which became a standard botanical reference work throughout the Islamic world and medieval Europe. Although Islam discouraged "image" making, the portrayal of floral, herbal, and vegetable motifs was permitted for scholarly purposes and for architectural decoration. Abu Hanifa al-Dinavari (*c.*820–95), the so-called "father" of Arab botany, collected all known botanical material from encyclopedias, herbals, and poetry and combined them with Bedouin stories that were transmitted orally. In the 11th century al-Biruni (d. 1030), noted the geometric alignment of flower parts and petals while studying the medicinal properties of plants.

The Caliph of Baghdad set an example for subsequent royal palaces, such as Samarra on the Tigris 70 miles north of Baghdad, where the 'Abbasid court moved in 835. Originally intended to house the caliph's Turkish army which had caused riots in Baghdad, Samarra remained the capital until 892 when it was abandoned to the desert and drifting sands. The geographer al-Ya'qubi, writing in 889 toward the end of its occupancy, reported that the whole land was converted to gardens "for the upper class" with palaces, and playgrounds for polo, which was already a national pastime. Underground canals carried water from the river further north. Waterwheels, powered by oxen or by trained ostriches, pumped the water into smaller rills, making it possible for gardens to have vast ornamental pools. Those in

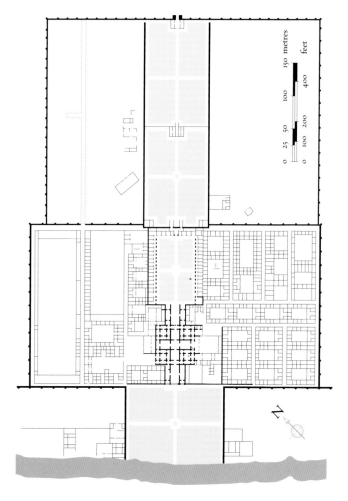

♦ A reconstruction, ABOVE, of the quadripartite groundplan of the garden of the 9th-century Balkuwara Palace in Samarra.
♦ Elaborate brickwork, OPPOSITE, on a Seljuk tomb tower in Damghan shows kufic inscriptions from the Koran.

the caliph's palace measured 218 yards square (as vast as the 19th-century Menara water tank, still to be seen surrounded by olive groves in Marrakesh, its green-tiled pavilion built in 1866). The Jausaq al-Khaqani extended to 428 acres of which 69 acres were gardens.

The court poet al-Bohtori described a Samarra palace called as-Sabi:

> And the stream being replenished with gushing water,
> glittering like a luminous sword
> When it burst into the middle of the beautiful pond
> its marble colours the water would assume
> And the waterwheels rotate with no animal or plough
> but with ostriches
> These gardens make us long ardently for Paradise and
> thus we eschew more sins and shun evil deeds.

Twentieth-century excavations have revealed the foundations of many palaces and gardens in Samarra, one of which was the Balkuwara Palace, built between 849 and 860. Constructed of unbaked brick, the buildings deteriorated quickly after the city was abandoned, leaving the outline of the gardens to be discovered more than a thousand years later. Inside the urban complex a series of courtyards was raised one above the other until they reached the main throne room, with a flat roof that afforded views over the plains and surrounding buildings. Quartered by intersecting paths and water rills, the garden, with a large central pool overlooking the river, was constructed on a strict axial pattern, one of the earliest examples of the *chahar bagh* concept in the Muslim era.

The magnificence of Samarra was short-lived, but sufficient ruins have survived in the dry desert atmosphere for archaeologists to make detailed measurements of foundations. The estates and palace gardens with vast water tanks became a stimulus to later developments both throughout the Middle East and in further outposts of Islam, such as Spain and India. The palatial garden city of Madinat az-Zahra (see page 155) outside Cordoba, built in the 10th century, was in part modeled on Samarra, its main palace, with arcaded pavilions facing large water tanks, reminiscent of the Balkuwara Palace.

By the 9th century 'Abbasid power was dissipated among minor dynasties, who asserted their authority in different regions and whose rulers made their own contribution to the development of palace and garden history on Persian soil. Saffarids, Samanids, and Buyids followed in rapid succession. The 10th-century poet Daqiqi describes the garden of the Samanid king in the city of Bukhara across the River Oxus (now the Amu-Darya), admiring its layout, the beauty of its trees, and the fragrance of its flowers.

The Buyids, from the Caspian Sea provinces, the first Iranian Muslim dynasty to re-unite western Persia, revived Sasanian monumental palace architecture on native soil during the 10th century. 'Azod ad-Douleh made his capital at Shiraz from 945, calling himself "King of Kings" (*Shahanshah* in Persian; *Malek al-Moluk* in Arabic). He was responsible for a palace outside the old city, described by the contemporary Arab historian Moqaddesi as situated among *bostans*. It had two stories with 360 rooms and around it were laid out orchards and *ashjar* (groves); streams flowed through the rooms and *revaq* (arcaded courts), bringing the outside garden into the interior, as was often depicted in later miniature paintings.

The period of successive Iranian dynasties came to an end with the Ghaznavids (977–1186), who established a seat of power at Ghazna in eastern Afghanistan, their rule extending into Khorasan in Persia. The court of Soltan Mahmud (998–1030) was celebrated by the contemporary poet Farrokhi. No longer firmly enclosed, the garden described is open to the countryside with the wild mountainside receiving as much praise as the garden. Trees, flowers, and birds figure largely, combined with the drama of wind, rain, and storms. In his *Divan* Farrokhi wrote:

The weather is improving and the snow is melting on
the mountain,

The banners of spring are raised on the slopes.
The earth in its happiness seems to be the wide heavens,
and the wide heavens are a blooming garden.
At night the flowers in the garden are like a gardener's
lantern . . .
Each lover takes wine in hand and strolls towards
the garden with a seductive beauty.

His images of spring and joy give rise to thoughts of love:

I have an idol whose face in December is a rose bush and
a Judas tree blooming together.
Whether spring comes or not, the flowers in my beloved's face
will not wither.
In my idol's face I have a new sort of garden, which unlike
other gardens, will never be saddened by time.

The Seljuks, a clan of Oghuzz Turks who settled first in Transoxiana and Bukhara, took over from the Ghaznavids in Khorasan in the middle of the 11th century. Within a few years, they entered Baghdad, where their leader was proclaimed successor of the Prophet and Lord of all Muslims by the last of the 'Abbasid caliphs. They were responsible for many of the great monuments of the 11th and 12th centuries, including the four-*ayvan* plan for both mosques and *madraseh* (religious schools) and a more three-dimensional structural approach to architecture. They used complex brick patterning in geometric designs, schemes realized by local

craftsmen. The Seljuks were also the first to use the Arabic word *bagh* to describe the entity of palace and garden.

The third Seljuk ruler, Malek Shah (1072–92), who was advised by his vizier, Nezam al-Molk, patron of Omar Khayyam, built four gardens in Isfahan, each a thousand *jarib* (about 2½ acres), beginning the city's long association with gardens. A contemporary poet described fruit trees and roses growing next to cypresses beside a stream, but does little to bring to life the garden's overall appearance, his purpose being to flatter the king and, by praising his gardens, to confirm the prestige of the royal owner. The Bagh-e Bakr, fragrant with narcissus, myrtle, and saffron, the shaded seats fanned by cooling breezes, was made even more pleasant by the cooing of doves. The Bagh-e Falasan had a high-built pavilion commanding a fine view over the garden in which there were grapevines and brimming streams. The Bagh-e Karan was still in existence in the 14th century to be described by Hafez (*c.*1324–89) in one of his *ghazals* (romantic odes): "Though a hundred rivers flow before my eyes, Zenderud [the river flowing through Isfahan] and the Bagh-e Karan shall linger in my memory." It was planted with fruit trees and rows of cypresses and pines, with one pavilion overlooking the river, today called the Zayandeh Rud.

Although they were great builders and innovators—they introduced water mills for paper making, which had a decisive influence on the way in which arts developed after and around 1200—the Seljuks never established order in their dominions. In particular, they failed to check the growing power of the *Hashishiyun* (Assassins), founded by Hasan Sabah (1040–1124). At the height of their powers under 'Ala ad-Din, known to the west as the "Old Man or Sheikh of the Mountain," the dreaded *Hashishiyun* spread their net from Syria to Khorasan province, sending out killers from their fortress of Alamut north of Qazvin to murder political and religious figures and striking terror throughout the regions, with Malek Shah's vizier among their victims.

In his *Travels* Marco Polo relates the story of the Valley of the Assassins as it was told to him in the north, many years after Hulagu had besieged the mountain fortress in 1256 and 'Ala ad-Din had been put to death by his own men. Marco Polo heard how the sheikh had created "the biggest and

◆ *The Alamut valley,* ABOVE, *northeast of Qazvin, the site of the remote castle of Hasan Sabah.* ◆ OPPOSITE *An almond, a cypress, a plane tree, and a young white-stemmed poplar establish the traditional garden scene for a princely reception in the countryside, where flowers bloom in a meadow in front of a canopied dais. In all twenty-two people play music and amuse the prince while a cook roasts a meal on a spit. This early-17th-century miniature is set in a frame showing wild animals and birds treated with gold leaf.*

most beautiful garden that was ever seen" in a valley between two mountains and had used the sacred concept of the paradise garden as revealed to Mohammad in the Koran to dupe "all the youths of the country from twelve to twenty" into carrying out missions of murder. The secret garden was "planted with all the finest fruits in the world" and contained "the most splendid mansions and palaces that were ever seen, ornamented with gold and with likenesses of all that is beautiful on earth." And "because Mahomet assured the Saracens that those who go to Paradise will have beautiful women to their hearts' content to do their bidding, and will find there rivers of wine and milk and honey and water," the garden had four conduits and there were "fair ladies there and damsels, the loveliest in the world, unrivaled at playing every sort of instrument and at singing and dancing." "Now mark what follows," Marco Polo continues:

> He [the sheikh] used to put some of these youths in this Paradise, four at a time, or ten, or twenty, according as he wished. And this is how he did it. He would give them draughts [of a hashish concoction] that sent them to sleep on the spot. Then he had them taken and put in the garden, where they were awakened. When they awoke and found themselves in there … they believed they were really in Paradise. And the ladies and damsels stayed with them all the time, singing and making music for their delight and ministering to all their desires … When they awoke they believing they had been in Paradise and longing for it, were willing to go out and kill, and looked forward to the day of their going. In this way he was able to send out the Assassins where ever he might wish and that if they died on their mission they would go to Paradise all the sooner.

During the last decades of Seljuk rule under Soltan Sanjar (1118–57), marauders from Central Asia increasingly threatened the Persian world and it was they who eventually overpowered it.

The mausoleum of Ne'matollah Vali

◆ The Sufi shrine, with courts, ayvans, LEFT, and dome chamber, is still remarkable for its harmonious beauty and religious atmosphere. ◆ Sacred geometry in the second courtyard, BELOW: an octagonal within a cruciform pool (empty of water for repairs). ◆ Calligraphy, geometry, and foliation decorate the door into the first courtyard, OPPOSITE, where a pool, shaded by cypresses, provides a place for pilgrims to rest before prayer.

Aramgah-e Shah Ne'matollah Vali, the grave of the Sufi divine and poet who founded a dervish order, is a place of pilgrimage in Mahan, on the edge of the Dasht-e Lut. The earliest buildings date to the lifetime of Ne'matollah Vali, who died in 1431. They were beautified by Shah 'Abbas I and embellished by the Qajars.

The grave is set in a series of peaceful garden enclosures, each of which is dominated by shade-giving cypresses around pools that serve for ablutions. In the first courtyard to the east, recesses around the reflecting rectangular pool provided resting places for weary travelers. In the second enclosure, the water feature is cruciform in shape and the central pool is an octagon. Behind the shrine there is a further courtyard with a small square pool, its corners marked by cypresses. Beds of flowers and potted geraniums edge the water.

5 Luxurious encampments

"The real gardens and flowers are within,
they are in man's heart, not outside."

Rumi *The Masnavi* Book IV

 IN THE 13TH CENTURY THE CIV-
ILIZED WORLD, CULTIVATED BY
ISLAM FOR SEVEN CENTURIES,
was ravaged by Mongol hordes. They descended on the
western and eastern Iranian lands ruled by the Seljuks and
on the remaining territories of the 'Abbasid caliph in Baghdad, eventually reaching the shores of the eastern Mediterranean. Under Genghiz Khan, cities in Afghanistan and
eastern Iran were destroyed and plundered, and the citizens
were massacred. Raiding parties damaged ancient *qanats* and
filled wells with sand. Unwatered fields returned to desert.
The eastern part of this vast empire remained under direct
rule of the Great Khan, the successor to Genghiz, while the
rest was parceled out into subordinate khanships. Between
1256 and 1265 Hulagu Khan, Genghiz' grandson, extin-
guished the Caliphate in Baghdad, his hordes pillaging the
city and breaking down the banks of canals. The deltas re-
verted to malarial swamps, bringing famine and disease to a
civilization which had existed for 4,000 years.

Although much that was beautiful and sacred was obliterated, as the Mongols settled down to become yet another
Iranian dynasty, architectural and artistic development continued. Palaces and luxurious gardens inspired poets to
write *ghazals* in which the gardens are symbols of worldly
success, and flowers and fruit are metaphors for both spiritual and romantic love. Persian painters created exquisite
miniatures in which legendary heroes and heroines people
walled gardens complete with pavilions, pools, flowers, and
trees. Because of the vast areas covered by the "golden
hordes," new cultural contacts were established between
Europe and the frontiers of distant China.

Hulagu was a destroyer, but his successor, Abaqa, was a builder. In the summer palace he built in the 1270s at Takht-e Soleiman, the sacred site of the Sasanian Zoroastrian Shiz in the uplands of Kurdistan, he incorporated surviving Sasanian structures. To the east of Khosrou II's ceremonial *ayvan* he created a further three to make one of the largest courtyards in Persian architecture (about 130 × 160 yards), with the lake as a pool in its center.

In 1302 Ghazan Khan (1295–1304) made a garden which reflected the nomadic way of life, the Bagh-e 'Adalat (Garden of Justice) near Tabriz. The square, walled enclosure, with a Golden Pavilion and Golden Throne, as well as towers, baths, and lofty buildings, was planned "to provide a pleasant and agreeable meadow for the sojourn of the emperor" where streams were fed by water stored in tanks and cisterns. Outside the walls, avenues of willows around the edge provided passageways for the ordinary people.

In 1369 Timur (1335–1405), a Central Asian prince known in the West as Tamerlane, declared himself heir to Genghiz Khan and seized power in Samarkand in Transoxiana, spending the rest of the century expanding his empire to include the whole of Iran, some of India, and part of Russia, with cities such as Tabriz, Baghdad, Aleppo, and Delhi under his control. He destroyed the old trade routes of the Iranian plateau on which centuries of prosperity had relied. But Timur was also a builder and spared the lives of skilled artisans and craftsmen in the vanquished cities, where he built palaces and gardens. In Samarkand he created buildings embellished with tile work and gardens on a vast scale,

which he allowed the populace to enjoy: "the citizens, rich and poor, went to walk therein and found no retreat more wonderful or beautiful than those and no resting place more agreeable and secure, and its sweetest fruits were common to all." We even have the name of one of the planters of trees, Shahab ad-Din Ahmad Zardakashi, but know nothing more of his life and skills.

Timur's style of garden making was to influence 16th-century gardens in both Safavid Persia and at the courts of the Mughal emperors on the northern plains of India. The basic format of the walled oasis remained the same but gardens acquired a more public ambience as settings for festivities and royal receptions, with sumptuous tents and awnings pitched on lawns of clover in orchards watered by streams. These luxurious encampments inspired poets to write *ghazals* set in gardens where roses bloomed and nightingales sang, and Persian painters to create delicate miniatures of walled gardens with sumptuous carpets laid on flower-studded grass, shaded by trees, pavilions, and canopies.

Samarkand lay in a great fertile plain, the fields watered by canals drawn from the River Zarafshan to the north, an area of hot rainless summers and very cold winters. Ruy Gonzalez de Clavijo, an envoy from Henry III in faraway Castile, arrived on the plain on August 31 1404 at the end of summer, the driest time of the year when dust storms frequently blew over the city, having taken fifteen months on the journey from Spain. Nevertheless, he recorded that "only a mountainous height of trees" indicated the city in the distance, and "the houses embowered among them

◆ PRECEDING PAGES *The frontispiece to the* Zafar-nameh (Book of Victory) *of Sharaf ad-Din 'Ali Yazdi, written in 1424, shows Timur at a reception in a royal pleasure garden on the occasion of his accession in 1369. Beneath a sumptuous canopy, the heir to the great Genghiz Khan, and lord of Samarkand, holds court in a flower-studded orchard.* ◆ *The awning and raised dais depicted in the mid-16th-century miniature,* OPPOSITE, *are reminiscent of Clavijo's descriptions of Timur's garden encampments at Samarkand in the first years of the century. A central pool and straight water channel contrast with the undulating stream in the landscape which winds around the garden, planted with symbolic cypress and almond trees. The painting, illustrating Nezami's* Khamseh, *dates to the reign of Shah Tahmasp.*

remain invisible." Clavijo arrived in Cairo, one of a series of villages named after the greatest cities in the Muslim world—Damascus, Baghdad, Soltanieh, and Shiraz—that encircled Samarkand. There, in an enclosure "full of fruit trees of all kinds" where "six large tanks" fed a "great stream of water [that] flows from one end of the orchard to the other," he awaited the Emperor's summons. Beyond the orchard was a walled vineyard, likewise surrounded by "rows of tall and shady trees." "Avenues of trees, very lofty and shady, which appear as streets, for they are paved to be like platforms," quartered the orchard where deer and pheasants roamed. On the top of a hill in the center, built up with clay and encircled with deep ditches, were built several beautiful palaces, reached by bridges and stairways.

On September 8, the Spanish ambassador was finally summoned to meet the Emperor in another garden enclosure outside the city. At Delgosha (Heart's Ease), reached through a high gateway "most beautifully ornamented with tile work in gold and blue," Timur, aged seventy and almost blind (he died the following February), reclined on embroidered mattresses upon a raised dais beneath a portal. In front of him a fountain threw a column of water into the air which landed in a basin where red apples floated. In the surrounding orchards "there were pitched many tents the walls of which were of silk stuff or the like." Within days Timur moved to the Bagh-e Chenar (Plane Tree Garden) and on the 15th to another, "a place of great beauty," in which he provided a feast for the ambassadors. At its center was a fine palace built in

the shape of a cross. The Bagh-e Nou was the most sumptuous, its vast buildings ornamented with gold and blue tiles. On September 23 Timur moved to yet another garden where each ambassador was presented with a robe of golden bro-

◆ *Outside a profusely planted walled garden, Prince Homay waits at the castle gates, where pollarded willows grow beside the stream. Painted by Jonayd in Baghdad in 1396, the scene is from the* Divan *of* Khwaju Kermani. *With a newly invented script by Mir 'Ali Tabrizi, this manuscript is one of the great monuments of Persian painting.*

cade, a customary gift to those favoured by the king. Timur moved into the city of Samarkand on September 29.

By October 6, Timur was planning a great feast in the royal camp. Innumerable tents, with awnings of embroidered linen, open to the sky and catching the breezes, had been pitched side by side next to the River Zarafshan. A huge square tent for the Emperor, lined with crimson tapestry, supported a central dome. Clavijo describes many more tented enclosures as the settings for feasts given by Timur and also by the wife of his eldest son, during which many people, including the princesses, got drunk on the wine.

Records by local witnesses—Sharaf ad-Din 'Ali Yazdi writing in 1424 and Ibn 'Arabshah in 1436—combined with Clavijo's contemporary report, indicate that Timur created at least eleven pleasure gardens. For the Bagh-e Shomal (Northern Garden), begun in 1396, he ordered architects from Fars, Azerbaijan, and Baghdad to compete to build four corner pavilions and a central palace with walls of marble and glazed tile. Other walls were to be decorated with frescoes. In 1404 he directed architects from Damascus to build a new and magnificent palace in a garden south of the Bagh-e Shomal. Ibn 'Arabshah describes a meadow a mile outside the city as "a carpet of emerald, on which are sprinkled diverse gems of hyacinth," probably the Khaneh-e Gol (House of Flowers), in the direction of Kesh lay Shahr-e Sabz (City of Green), in which the Palace of the Black Throne was situated.

Babur (1483–1530), a descendant of Timur through his father and of Genghiz Khan through his mother, visited Samarkand while still young and impressionable, nearly a hundred years after Timur's death. He was inspired by the gardens he saw there, including the Bagh-e Chenar and gardens made by Timur's grandson, Ulogh Beg, to make his own fabulous gardens in and around Kabul and on the dusty plains of northern India. (One of Ulogh Beg's gardens, now inside the expanded city, was excavated by Professor Galina Pugachenkova in 1941.) The Chahar Bagh, created by Ahmad Mirza in the late 15th century, pleased Babur most:

[The garden] lies overlooking the whole of Qulba Meadow, on the slope below the Bagh-e Maidan. Moreover it is arranged symmetrically, terrace above terrace, and is planted with beautiful *narvan* [elm] and cypresses and white poplar. A most agreeable sojourning place, its one defect is the want of a large stream.

In his memoirs, the *Babur-nameh*, he wrote that "few towns in the whole habitable world are so pleasant as Samarkand." He established a dynasty of emperors who were to create some of the most beautiful gardens in the world.

Timur's son, Shah Rokh (1408–47) moved his capital to Herat, where he created a garden of 100 acres, with a pool, and flowerbeds of red tulips and roses. Under royal patronage Herat became a glittering center for both science and the arts, which flourished there as never before. Contemporary poetry and early miniatures painted in Herat's heyday make it clear that by the 15th century gardens and flowers had earned a special place in contemporary culture. The first Persian work to offer constructive advice on garden layouts was composed there in 1515. The *Ershad az-zara'a*, a treatise on husbandry by Qasem ibn Yusof, recommends ideas that were later adopted in Safavid Persia and by Babur and successive Mughal emperors. Qasem, a scholar of mathematics and topography, writes about soil, choosing crops, auspicious times for planting grains, vegetables, and vines, transplanting trees, grafting fruit trees, and the design of the *chahar bagh* and its pavilions. He emphasizes shade-giving trees, preferring the Samarqandi poplar (the white-stemmed *Populus alba* f. *pyramidalis*) to the pine, fruit-bearing trees as specimens or grouped in four plots, with flowers in the same manner, and clover as a substitute for grass. Scholars who have interpreted the work have identified the plants as far as possible. Qasem obtained his information from Mirak Sayyid Ghiyas, a renowned garden builder in late-Timurid Herat, who finally with his son, the designer of Homayun's tomb in Delhi, joined Babur in India in 1529.

In Herat artists were able to paint delicate miniatures in real gardens, portraying living plants in the scenes from pre-Mongol literature including Ferdousi's 11th-century epic *Shahnameh* or "Book of Kings" and Nezami's 12th-century romantic poems. The miniatures show walled gardens set in landscapes with streams and rills, flowers and trees, and carpets, patterned with floral decoration, set out for entertaining. Although the flowers were taken from life, gardens were of the mind rather than actual layouts, with human beings acting out romantic and legendary scenes. Many of the trees and flowers portrayed provide a source of botanical detail for the period. Often the heroes and heroines sat on carpets woven with decorative trees and flowers. No "garden" carpets survive from the 15th century, but these pictures confirm their earlier existence.

Persia contributed to the world's art a type of painting which is unique. Although the scale of the jewel-like paintings is so small, often executed with a single hair from the tail of a squirrel with the most delicate precision, the portrayal is so exact as to bear considerable enlargement, which can reveal detail hardly visible to the naked eye. Executed entirely in color but without light or shade, the miniatures are painted like a bird's-eye view, to be seen from a certain elevation, allowing objects at different distances to be visible, while a carpet is drawn as if on a flat plane. Often there is a backcloth of rising ground, with slopes convenient for half hiding and half revealing out-of-scale figures for dramatic effect. The hills are portrayed with flowering plants, suitably enlarged to be recognizable in spite of their distance. The whole picture is set off by a sky which may be of gold or azure blue. Persian paintings use a brilliant palette of pure hues, unmuddied by the presence of shadows.

Poetry has a long tradition in Persia, transcending the bounds of literature and literacy as a serious manifestation, a window through which to regard the world. Its origins date back to Zoroastrian works written in the 9th century BC. Edward Fitzgerald's 1859 translation of the 12th-century

◆ Khosrou is seen feasting, sitting on a flowery carpet in a meadow of wild flowers, ABOVE. Musicians play to accompany the feast. Besides being designed as "gardens," carpets were often patterned with "everlasting" flowers, which not only brought nature into the house but would also be used for al fresco meals. Carpets portrayed in miniatures pre-date any surviving Persian carpets. This miniature, one of thirty-eight in the series illustrating Nezami's Khamseh, *was painted by Mahmud in 1431 for Shah Rokh. ◆ Sa'di's tomb in Shiraz, OPPOSITE, is surrounded by flowery gardens celebrating the poet's love of garden imagery.*

Rubaiyat of Omar Khayyam, in which man is exhorted to make merry "before we too into the Dust descend," is best known in the West. In Iran, however, Omar Khayyam is more celebrated for his philosophy, mathematics, and astronomy than for his poetic powers. There is a wealth of verse little known outside Iran that celebrates the beauties of gardens, the greatest being Ferdousi's *Shahnameh*. Part legend and partly based on historical fact, the story of the ancient shahs evokes the palace gardens of the Sasanian era, a time when Persia had its own empire. Within four hundred years these legendary tales, and those of Nezami's *Khamseh*, became subjects of beautiful miniatures in which garden pools, walled enclosures, flowers, and trees are the settings.

Unlike contemporary Western art where subject matter was taken from the Bible, the Persians, banned from using images and figure painting by the revelations of the Prophet, found their subjects in epic poetry and romance familiar to the spectator. Their designs were executed for princes and nobles. The mystical nature of medieval Persian poetry such as that of Rumi, Sa'di, Hafez, and Jami is revealed by showing Sufis (mystics) sitting in the open, alone or in conference. Later many of the miniaturists fled from austere religious persecution to India where they continued to portray the luxurious gardens of the Mughal emperors, in courts where Persian was still the official language.

Since the 11th century great poets have been considered as on the same level as great mystics, with Jalal ad-Din Rumi (d. 1273), founder of the Moulavi order of "whirling" dervishes, one of the greatest influences. His long poem in six books, *The Masnavi*, contains the basic teachings of the Sufis who draw inspiration from the shrines of renowned mystics of earlier centuries, hold that God and the world are one, the world being only an emanation of the deity: "God said, I was a hidden treasure and I desired to be discovered, so I created man in order that he might discover me."

In the 13th and 14th centuries, while other parts of Persia were being reduced to rubble and ashes, the two most beloved Persian poets, Sa'di (*c.* 1213–92) and Hafez (*c.* 1324–89),

whose mausoleums in Shiraz are still places of pilgrimage, brought renown to their birthplace. Both dwell on nature and gardens in their poetry.

The grave of Sa'di, a greater traveler than Hafez and as great a poet, lies at the entrance to a narrow valley with a natural deep spring. It is less visited than that of Hafez and the tombstone lies alone, surrounded by gardens with shady pines and cypresses. Sa'di's works are consulted for his morality—he preached moderation and concern for upright behavior in this life, and wrote with rapturous approval of his city:

> *Pleasant is the new year's outing, especially in Shiraz,*
> *Which turns aside the heart of the wanderer from his*
> *native land.*

Hafez's tomb garden

Shams ad-Din Mohammad—or Hafez, "he who knows the Koran by heart"—wrote some 600 *ghazals* (romantic odes), often using garden imagery to express sentiments of romantic love and, above all, divine longing, with "wine" and "drunkenness" as metaphors for immersion in the love of God.

Among his works is a description of the Musalla pleasure ground, the site where his tomb was to be erected, watered by the stream of Roknabad, fed by *qanat*:

> *Bring, Cup-bearer, all that is left of*
> *thy wine*
> *In the Garden of Paradise vainly*
> *thou'lt seek*
> *The lip of the fountain of Roknabad*
> *And the bowers of Musalla where*
> *roses twine.*

A dome symbolizing eternity was erected over the tomb in the middle of the 15th century, but it was not until the regency of Karim Khan Zand that this became a mausoleum and a place of pilgrimage. He contributed an alabaster tombstone inscribed with some of the poet's own verses. Visitors can still, as they have for centuries, take the omens, or *fal*, by picking at random a page of Hafez's *Divan* or Collected Works, kept ready for this purpose.

The octagonal kiosk was constructed more recently. Other graves surround the main tomb. In spite of the crowds of pilgrims, the gardens, with blue-tiled pools and scented flowers, shaded by tall cypresses, are restful and atmospheric.

◆ *The poet's tomb lies in an octagonal kiosk,* ABOVE, *set in an immaculately maintained walled garden on the north bank of the river in Shiraz.* ◆ *The sixteen-pointed star on the ceiling of the dome,* OPPOSITE ABOVE. ◆ *Flowers, including plumbago and geraniums, planted in the pale-colored terracotta pots seen all over Persia, flank the steps of the mausoleum,* LEFT, *and surround the pool,* OPPOSITE BELOW *(illustrated on page 13).*

6   Triumphant gardens

"On either side of the road are symmetrical straight walls; and within the walls are gardens which, up to half-way along the avenue, belong to the king, and are kept for whoever wishes to go in and wander about."
Pietro della Valle

 THE SAFAVIDS CONTINUED TO MAKE GARDENS BASED ON THE QUADRIPARTITE *CHAHAR BAGH*. As well as enclosed sacred gardens, recalling the Biblical Garden of Eden and the Muslim Paradise for the faithful, they built secular royal pleasure gardens around tent-like reception halls, developments of Timurid paradise gardens where canopied pavilions were set in orchards watered by streams. Safavid palaces, built with a minimum of weight-bearing walls pierced with large windows, niches, and loggias, opened out at ground level into ample gardens for receptions and public entertainment, seeming insubstantial, almost ephemeral, in comparison with Sasanian architecture of a thousand years earlier.

Many Safavid gardens have almost disappeared or vanished completely. Fortunately, there are contemporary records of their lavish beauty to enliven those that do survive. Pietro della Valle, a nobleman from Rome who had undertaken a pilgrimage to the Holy Land in 1614, a form of Grand Tour which incorporated Turkey, Persia, and India, arrived in Isfahan in February 1617 and was later received by Shah 'Abbas I in the Caspian. The Spanish ambassador, Don Garcia de Silva Figueroa, visited Qazvin in June 1618. Thomas Herbert accompanied Charles I's ambassador, Sir Dodmore Cotton, to Persia to open up trade in raw silk in 1628, and recorded his impressions of Isfahan, Shiraz, and the Caspian. Sir John Chardin, to whom we owe the greatest debt, gave a lively picture of newly built Safavid palaces and gardens, and how they were used. Later visitors left copious accounts of gardens and 19th-century engravings portray their elegance and beauty even in decay.

EARLY SAFAVID GARDENS

At the age of fourteen Shah Isma'il Safavi (1499–1524), founder of the Safavid dynasty, was crowned at Tabriz, inheriting the palace and garden of Hasht Behesht (Eight Paradises) built for Uzun Hasan, ruler of the White Sheep Turkoman between 1466 and 1478. Situated on the outskirts of the city, the central part of the octagonal palace was covered with a great dome embellished with paintings. From accounts written by an Italian merchant who traveled between 1511 and 1520, we know that the palace stood in the center of a vast garden, enclosed by a wall with portals on the north, south, and east sides. The eastern entrance had galleries looking onto the garden and outward on the *maidan* (main square). In the southwest corner, a gallery had seats and columns of finest marble, in front of which was a "fountain full of water and 25 paces broad." Swans swam in the water tank and jasmine and roses grew around its edge.

Isma'il was a descendant of Sheikh Safi ad-Din of Ardabil in the northwest, a connection that appealed to his followers who considered him to be both a saint and a zealous warrior, "as brave as a peacock and stronger than any of his lords." He proclaimed the Shi'ite version of Islam and fought holy wars, establishing power over Iraq, Fars, Khorasan, and Hamadan. In his antagonism towards the Sunnis or more orthodox Muslims, he fostered the enmity of the Ottoman Turks and other Muslim countries west of Iran, as well as the Sunni Muslims of Central Asia, Afghanistan, and India.

Warlike pressure on Iran from without led to yet greater national fervor, united by Shah Isma'il's Safavids and the Shi'a faith, increasing the split between the two main branches of Islam. The division had arisen within a few years of Mohammad's death in AD 632 over who should succeed. Both branches followed the preachings of the Prophet Mohammad, with God's Word revealed in the Koran, and shared the Bible with Christianity and Judaism. All Muslims allow Jesus to be a prophet, second only to Mohammad in importance but not the Son of God. However, the Shi'ites believed that leadership should remain in the Prophet's family, choosing 'Ali, his cousin and

◆ PRECEDING PAGES *The view across the water tank from the main pavilion of the Chehel Sotun in Isfahan.* ◆ *Sufi mystics,* ABOVE, *discoursing and reading in a garden, sit beside a winding stream, flanked by blossoming almonds, that flows down the hillside. Hollyhocks, narcissus, and dark-flowered irises bloom on the slopes and beside the water. The miniature was painted by Qasim 'Ali in Herat in 1485.* ◆ OPPOSITE *Remnants of the garden constructed by Shah 'Abbas I around the mausoleum of Sheikh Safi ad-Din at Ardabil in northwest Iran.*

son-in-law, as legitimate successor and the first Imam, while
the Sunnis chose Abu Bakr, the Prophet's closest companion. The split widened when Ali's son, Hosein, was brutally
killed at Karbala in southern Iraq in 680. His role was
passed on through the family until the twelfth Imam disappeared in 873. Since the Safavid period, Persia has been
committed to the Shi'a faith, which accounts for only ten
per cent of the Muslim community in the Islamic world,
whereas the Sunnis form the majority.

According to tradition, in 1504 notables entertained Shah
Isma'il in a walled garden enclosure at Bagh-e Fin outside
Kashan, on the edge of the great salt desert in the eastern
foothills of the Zagros. It is one of the most beautiful
gardens in Persia, indeed holding its own among the great
gardens of the world, built in the faultless style of an extended quadripartite garden. With ample water, brought by
qanat from the mountains and stored in a great cistern above
the garden, the fountains work by gravity, bubbling through
turquoise-tiled channels between ancient cypresses, probably planted in the 16th or 17th century. Later Shah 'Abbas I,
who is buried in Kashan, developed a royal residence, bathhouses, and a central pavilion.

The second Safavid ruler, Shah Tahmasp, reigned from
1524 to 1576, suffering defeats at the hands of the Turkish
ruler Soleiman the Magnificent, his troops of tribal horse-
men no match for the famed Ottoman janissaries with their
muskets and artillery. The Ottomans pressed on as far as
Tabriz, taking over Iraq. Tahmasp moved his capital from
Tabriz to Qazvin, ruling there over a sophisticated court
where he entertained the exiled Mughal emperor, Homayun,
as well as an early emissary from the court of Queen
Elizabeth, Anthony Jenkinson. Shah Tahmasp's architects
extended the city of Qazvin with wide avenues flanked by
trees and waterways. When Don Garcia de Silva Figueroa
and his entourage visited in June 1618, they were led through:

> a broad alley lined with cypresses and plane trees,
> then in the middle and to the right they took another

smaller alley heavily covered by trees and came to a
very beautiful and large pool which was more than 150
yards square, in the middle of which stood a pretty
pavilion open on all sides.

A group of gardens called Sa'adatabad (Abode of Felicity),
around the Chehel Sotun Palace, the Doulat Khaneh and
the 'Ali Qapu, faced the great square, the Maidan-e Asb,
which was used for polo and public receptions. The garden,
divided geometrically in traditional fashion, had covered
pavilions, *ayvans* with a great *talar* behind, and central pools.

Bagh-e Fin

The magical Garden of Fin was laid out on an extended form of the *chahar bagh*, with a primary water axis from the monumental gateway leading the eye through the central pavilion to the top of the garden. A secondary axis cut the left-hand part of the garden in half with the water source, a brimming pool also lined with turquoise tiles, at the upper south end. Water feeds into this pool from a vast cistern outside the walls, kept full from a mountain *qanat*. A series of transverse water axes, narrow runnels opening out into wider basins, and raised walkways marching in dappled sunlight between dark scented cypresses make this garden uniquely beautiful.

The Bagh-e Fin is commonly dated to the reign of Shah 'Abbas, but we know that the walled enclosure existed in 1504 when it was the scene of a meeting between Shah Isma'il and his notables. Shah 'Abbas I almost certainly was responsible for adding buildings which were used to accommodate him and his court as they traveled through the country. It was visited by Shah 'Abbas II in 1659. The turquoise-tiled water rills, their bubble fountains still operating by gravity, and the venerable cypresses seen today date to the 17th century, although the tilework has been restored. The original buildings which were at the central crossing of the water rills disappeared and were replaced by Fath 'Ali Shah between 1799 and 1834. The Prime Minister of Persia, Mirza Taqi Khan, was murdered here in 1852 in the bathhouse inside the garden on the left of gateway by order of the young Naser ad-Din Shah.

◆ *Looking from calm water and still reflections in the central pavilion's shadowy interior,* ABOVE, *to bubbling jets in bright sunlight towards one of the garden's side buildings. Golab (rose water), still prized in Iran, is sold in the pavilion.* ◆ *Descending pools and rills,* TOP LEFT, *lined with turquoise tiles and linked by water shutes, lead to the main cypress-lined axis (page 93 overleaf).* ◆ *Constructed on the foundations of a Safavid building, the pavilion was replaced by Fath 'Ali Shah between 1799 and 1834 and has floral decorations,* TOP RIGHT, *typical of the Qajar period.* ◆ *Narrow watercourses beside the high perimeter walls run round rectangular basins of still, reflecting water,* OPPOSITE, *overhung by plane trees on the garden's western side.*

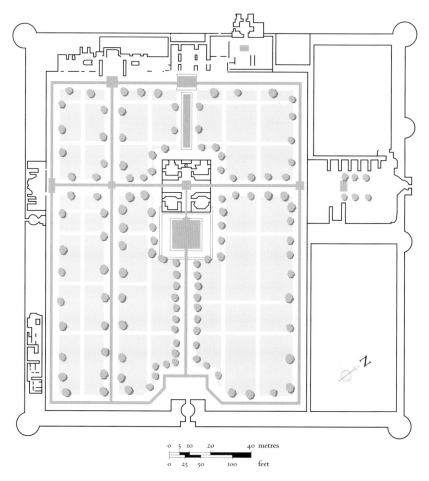

0 5 10   20   40 metres

0   25   50   100   feet

• The chahar bagh *layout, dating to the 16th century, extends in a series of squares and rectangles over 6½ acres,* ABOVE, *with the pavilion and a square basin in the center.* • *A rectangular pool,* ABOVE LEFT, *at the top of the garden, defines the axis behind the pavilion.* • *The broad central alley,* OPPOSITE ABOVE, *is shaded by 400-year-old cypress trees. Water, bubbling in rills and glistening in shafts of sunlight, is the element that has kept the paradise garden alive for four centuries.* • *Tall cypresses,* OPPOSITE BELOW LEFT, *cast shade over most of the garden, and grass grows in place of the shrub roses, pomegranates, jasmine, lilac, and spring-flowering bulbs that would have been grown originally.* • *A party of schoolgirls,* OPPOSITE BELOW RIGHT, *descends on the garden like a flock of chattering birds.*

"THE GREAT SOPHY"

Shah 'Abbas I (1587–1629), whose military successes, combined with achievements in the arts of peace, earned him the title "the Great," inherited from Shah Tahmasp a nation with threatening neighbors. He rapidly regained power over the eastern province of Khorasan, which the Uzbek Turks had invaded, and recovered Azerbaijan, Armenia, and Georgia from the Ottomans. Distrusting the Qizilbash tribal chiefs on whom previous Safavid rulers had depended for armed support, he built up an army from the population of many of the vanquished territories, raising money to pay them by establishing a system of crown lands which brought in sufficient income. He expanded trade and contacts with foreign courts and consolidated his Shi'ite legitimacy, building mosques and shrines all over the country and promoting them, in particular that of the Eighth Imam at Mashad, by making personal pilgrimages there on foot.

'Abbas's extensive road system, punctuated by many hundreds of caravanserais a day's journey apart, enabled his court to move throughout the country in grand style, strengthening the royal image, controlling the political behavior of the population, and discouraging possible sources of rebellion. Reputedly he built a causeway from Isfahan to the Caspian shore, where, connecting his new palaces, it was raised above the marshland.

It was 'Abbas's custom to create gardens wherever he could make use of them on his travels. Della Valle mentions one such in Tehran and Herbert gives us a tantalizing description of a garden that must have lain between Isfahan and the Caspian coast. The oasis town of Tajabad (its exact site unidentified) was located in a desert area, where a terraced garden was watered by *qanat*:

◆ *The old trade routes across the Iranian plateau are laced with caravanserai,* ABOVE, *many of which were constructed during the reign of Shah 'Abbas I.* ◆ *Within monumental walls,* OPPOSITE, *pilgrims and merchants, and their animals, were offered overnight protection.*

♦ PRECEDING PAGES *The early Safavid Fort of Tarq, on the road between Murchehkhurd and Natanz, is set above a natural spring and surrounded by verdant orchards and tall poplar trees.* ♦ *Pigeon towers,* ABOVE, *in the towns and countryside around Isfahan, first mentioned by Ibn Battuta in the 14th century, were built of brick, coated with lime, and resembled small forts. Hollow niches were provided for nesting and the manure was used to fertilize field crops, especially melons. The engraving is by Grelot who accompanied Sir John Chardin on his first visit to Persia.* ♦ *The fanciful view of Isfahan,* OPPOSITE, *also drawn and engraved by Grelot between 1660 and 1670, shows the city lying in a fertile plain between the desert and the Zagros Mountains. Shah 'Abbas's buildings are hardly identifiable, but the minarets must belong to the Masjed-e Shah (today the Imam Mosque), completed in 1629, its dome so high, wrote Chardin, "that coming from Kashan it could be seen a good dozen miles away."*

The garden is north from the house yet adjoining it [writes Herbert], it has severall descents, each part giving eightie paces, and seventy broad, this is watered by a cleare rivolet (tho little) by whose vertue it abounds in Damask Roses and other flowers, plentie of broad spreading Chenars (which is like our beech) with Pomegranates, Peaches, Apricockes, Plummes, Apples, Pears and Cherries ... it enjoys a Hot-House well built and paved with white Marble, and these are the rarer, because they are seated and walled about, in a large even Plaine rich in nothing but salt and sand.

ISFAHAN OR
"HALF THE WORLD"

Of all the great Shah's achievements, the finest was the rebuilding of Isfahan, a city of such beauty and richness as to rival any other of its time, its glittering domes, tiled with floral arabesques, towering above wide shaded avenues and terraced gardens. In 1598 Shah 'Abbas moved the imperial capital from Qazvin to Isfahan and for the next hundred years the royal city was reputed to be the most beautiful in the world, a center of commerce visited by merchants, ambassadors, and travelers from the West and from furthest Asia. The site was ancient—Isfahan is mentioned on Babylonian cuneiform tablets from the first millennium BC—and set 5,220 feet up on the Iranian plateau, ringed by rugged mountains. The land was rich, long cultivated, and fertilized by pigeon droppings collected in towers, noted by the 14th-century traveler Ibn Battuta from Tangier. The only major river on the plateau, the Zayandeh Rud, watered the fertile fields before emptying itself in the heat of the eastern desert. A torrent in winter and spring with water from melting snows, the river dried to a trickle in summer, thus encouraging the building of underground cisterns to service Shah 'Abbas's garden city.

Situated between mountains and the desert, Isfahan was a natural halting place for caravans preparing to cross the plateau to the north and east, besides being almost halfway between the Caspian coastline in the north and Fars and Shiraz in the south. Thomas Herbert describes the verdant

appearance of the city as a traveler approached, enlivened by tiled domes glittering in the bright Persian sunlight.

Gardens here for grandeur and fragour are such as no city in Asia outvies: which at a little distance from the city you would judge a forest, it is so large: but withal so sweet and verdant that you may call it another Paradise and Agreeable to the old report, *Horti Persarum erant amoenissimi* [the gardens of the Persians were most delightful].

Isfahan already had one of the great buildings of the world: the Friday or Jam'e Mosque, begun by the 'Abbasids in the 8th century, rebuilt by the Buyids in the 10th and by the Seljuks in the 11th and 12th centuries (restored and with additions up to the 18th century). Shah 'Abbas left the old city to the north, including the mosque, unchanged but connected it to the newly developed city area through the

bazaar. He imposed a new plan on the original, probably 15th-century Timurid park, an area filled with orchards, vineyards, and fields lying between the old town and the banks of the Zayandeh Rud. He shifted the focus to the south around a new, vast *maidan*, once an irregular market-place, laying out gardens behind his palace situated on its west side. A noble avenue, the Chahar Bagh, led down to the Zayandeh, the "life giving river," and over a new bridge, the Allahverdi Khan, to the south toward Shiraz. The main system of irrigation depended on a series of *madi* (canal) diverted from the river.

Shah 'Abbas encouraged immigration to Isfahan of peoples from Armenia and Georgia and of artisans from India and China, as well as European traders. He uprooted a whole Armenian community, 30,000 strong and mainly prosperous merchants from northwest Iran, to a suburb just south of the river, where they could practice their Christian religion and maintain their traditions of dress, while bringing trade to Isfahan.

As the population expanded, water had to be rationed in the summer. Just as a water master would control the distribution of water from *qanats* in a desert village, so the Shah's *mirab* was an important official supervising the Isfahan "rules" of water use.

• *The Mosque of Sheikh Lotfollah,* ABOVE, *is seen through water sprays arching over the central pool in the Maidan-e Shah. The great square, laid out by Shah 'Abbas in Isfahan, was used for markets, revues, and polo, the stone goalposts still visible at either end.* • *The de Bruyn engraving,* OPPOSITE, *published in 1718, shows merchants assembled with tents, and the water channel around the perimeter of the* maidan.

MAIDAN-E SHAH

To reflect the quasi-divine status of monarchy, an all-powerful sovereign at the center of the Persian universe, Shah 'Abbas centered his buildings on the immense Maidan-e Shah (Imperial Square, now the Maidan-e Naqsh-e Jahan). He converted the irregular site of the original marketplace into a formal rectangle, 623 × 194 yards, which is still one of the largest squares in the world—seven times the size

of St Mark's in Venice. Plenty of eyewitnesses give accounts of the Maidan-e Shah soon after it was laid out. One of the earliest was Pietro della Valle who arrived in Isfahan in February 1617 when building works were in progress. He describes the square as:

> completely surrounded by finely designed sym-metrical buildings, uninterrupted either by streets or anything else, made with large porticoes and floors underneath for shops with diverse merchandise set out in order ... and above with balconies and win-dows, filled with a thousand very pretty ornaments ... Around the Maidan, on four sides, flows a big channel of water, beautifully straight, lined with para-pets, and accompanied on the inside by a very smooth promenade made of stone. And beyond the flowing water, towards the porticoes, extends a very dense and even row of green trees, which, when they put forth their foliage in a few days' time, will, I believe, be the most beautiful sight in the world.

The square was covered with very fine shard for polo and other equine displays, suggesting that Herbert's description of "a large water tank at the centre" may be inaccurate:

> At the portal another, octangular, filled with pure water, which first glides round the inside of the Maydan through a stone course or channel, six foot [2m] deep and as many broad, which, after a pleasant murmur, drills [trickles] into this tank, whence it is sucked out by subterranean passages and distributed into private houses and gardens for use and refreshment.

Four great monuments occupied the four sides of the square. On the west was the 'Ali Qapu Pavilion (Lofty Gate or Sublime Portal), constructed in 1609 as a monumental gateway into the palace grounds. This was the Shah's ad-ministrative center, containing offices for dispensing justice and supervising the activities of the royal household, and rooms in which ambassadors, expected to offer substantial gifts, were received in great splendor, their duties to estab-lish profitable trade links, particularly in silk. A columned platform or verandah on the upper story provided the Shah with a place from which to view festivities in the *maidan* below, and allowed the people to see him sitting in state, thus forming a link between the sovereign and his people. A tank with three fountains splashed with glistening water raised by oxen working a rotating wheel. Built like a cube, the palace draws inspiration from Timurid tented pavilions rather than following the great traditions of Sasanian or Seljuk architecture, which are explicit in Safavid religious constructions seen across the square.

Behind the palace was the royal precinct, the ceremonial Talar Tavileh, lined with avenues of tall plane trees, the harem, and more gardens, including the Chehel Sotun (Pavilion of Forty Pillars), which was the largest and most lavish of those in the enclosure. The actual pavilion was built by 'Abbas II between 1642 and 1662. Set in a walled enclosure aligned with the *maidan*, it was constructed at the center of the quartered garden with a long reflecting pool stretching from its façade. Narrow watercourses set in stonework framed the building.

Opposite the 'Ali Qapu was the Shah's private place of worship, the Mosque of Sheikh Lotfollah, named for the father of one of Shah 'Abbas's wives who was a famous contemporary theologian. 'Ali Reza 'Abbasi, the greatest calligrapher of the Safavid period, decorated it with inscriptions, and its domed ceiling was a masterpiece of 17th-century Persian tile work, glowing with floral decoration in the light filtered through double grilled windows. On the north side of the square was the grand entrance to the Bazar Qaisarieh (Imperial Bazaar), a gateway decorated with tilework mosaic. To the south was Masjed-e Shah (Royal Mosque, today the Imam Mosque)—a symbol of spiritual faith—its entrance flanked by two turquoise minarets and its famous dome placed to the side to insure the *mehrab* faced toward Mecca. Begun in 1611, it was still unfinished at the time of Shah 'Abbas's death in 1629.

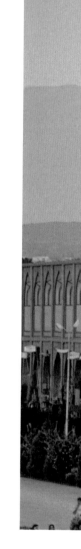

♦ ABOVE *The 'Ali Qapu Pavilion marked the entrance to Shah 'Abbas's palace complex and gardens. From the lofty open porch on the third floor, its ceiling supported by eighteen tree trunks sheathed with strips of wood, the Shah was visible to his subjects. He was also able to watch activities—such as revues of troops, entertainments, and polo matches taking place in the* maidan, *which was emptied of traders on state occasions.* ♦ *A corner of the Imam Mosque,* OPPOSITE ABOVE, *to the south of the maidan, showing the inner courtyard* ♦ *The Talar Tavileh,* OPPOSITE BELOW, *behind the 'Ali Qapu, was sumptuously decorated for the coronation of Shah Safi II in 1666 after the death of his father.*

Chehel Sotun

The Chehel Sotun was probably part of
the overall urban plan devised by Shah
'Abbas in 1598, its gardens stretching to
the square, although the pavilion itself
was built in the reign of his successor,
'Abbas II, and reconstructed in 1706 after
a fire. The pillars of plane tree wood
supporting the inlaid ceiling number
only twenty but reflected in the still water
there appear to be forty (alternatively the
word *chehel* can be translated as "many"
rather than "forty.") In the center of the
porch the four stone lions originally
spouted water into a marble basin and the
columns were pierced with holes so that
water shot straight into the pools which
they edged.

Located at the opposite end of the palace grounds from the harem, the pavilion
follows the Persian garden tradition of
establishing a close relationship between
the outside and inner rooms. The great
talar (porch), with slender towering columns supporting a painted ceiling, overlooks the pool. The *muqarnas* (stalactite)
vault in the entrance *ayvan* was originally
decorated with small pieces of glass

◆ *Four stone lions,* LEFT, *that once spouted water into a marble pool, support the
columns of the* talar *(page 104 overleaf).* ◆ *The pavilion looks out onto a large tank,*
OPPOSITE, *and originally was surrounded by a stone water rill. Column bases at the
four corners of the tank, and modern plantings of shrub roses around the edges, have
changed the ambience of the garden.* ◆ *The* ayvan, BELOW, *decorated with tiles and
shaded by trees, lies beyond the pavilion, opposite the modern entrance.*

that deflected light, while other panels contained Venetian mirrors presented by the Doge.

Much of the pavilion's interior is painted with panels, some of which date to the 18th-century Zand dynasty while others portray episodes from literature and show languid picnics in an idealized landscape—scenes typical of contemporary life in Safavid times, although much more recently restored. In the main hall four large paintings are of historic scenes, a battle against the Ottomans and three receptions for eastern rulers, showing wine drinking and dancing girls. In the side rooms, delicate floral and bird designs surround miniatures in poor repair.

The second coronation of 'Abbas II's son Soleiman (originally crowned Shah Safi II), witnessed by Chardin, took place in the pavilion in 1668. The reign of the indecisive and self-indulgent Soleiman had begun in 1666 with ill omens—famine, a plague of locusts, and threats of war in Afghanistan—and the general lack of firm government led to a perhaps more auspicious second "crowning." During Chardin's time the main hall was used for sumptuous banquets, lasting for three to four hours, the Shah seated on a square throne covered with fabrics embroidered with pearls, gold, and silver.

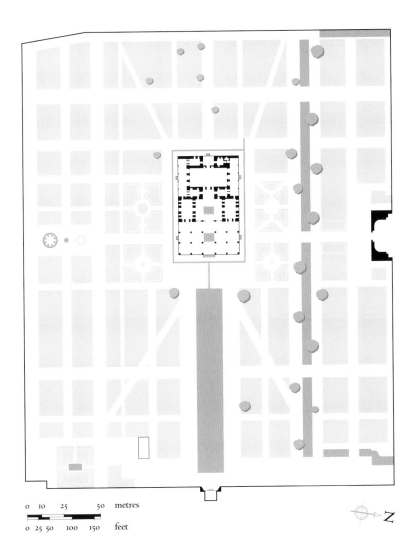

♦ *The Chehel Sotun pavilion,* OPPOSITE, *with water tank and high wooden* talar, *built by 'Abbas II, was reconstructed in Safavid style after a fire in 1706. Opening directly into the gardens, it was designed for receptions. Robert Byron attended a party in the Chehel Sotun in the 1930s: "Spread with carpets," he wrote, "lit with pyramids of lamps, and filled with several hundred people, the verandah looked enormous; its wooden pillars and painted canopy towered away into the night."* ♦ *The plan,* LEFT, *shows the long reflecting pool and the narrow watercourses surrounding the pavilion.* ♦ *Healthy native elm trees (*Ulmus minor*),* ABOVE LEFT, *line the main walks beside the tank and scented Brompton stocks,* ABOVE RIGHT, *grow in wooden-edged flowerbeds under the trees.*

0 10 25   50 metres

0 25 50   100   150 feet

N

THE GARDEN AVENUE

A noble avenue to the west of the *maidan*, the Chahar Bagh (Avenue of the Four Gardens), developed from a series of vineyards, ran from north to south. On either side, divided by descending water rills and flanked by elms and planes, were gardens with romantic and evocative names: the Garden of the Nightingale, the Mulberry Garden, the Garden of the Vineyard, the Garden of Barberries, and the Octagonal Garden. Della Valle noted the "symmetrical straight walls" along the avenue, enclosing gardens which, "up to half-way along the avenue, belong to the king, and are kept for whoever wishes to go in and wander about. Of the countless fruits growing there," he added, "whoever wishes can take some, with only a little favor to the gardener."

Garden pavilions of different construction and shape were painted and gilded, open on all sides in order that passersby could see more clearly into the gardens, admiring fine carpets laid out on the ground and clusters of flowers floating on pools. Della Valle considers the pavilions as having "very beautiful façades." They are "not very large," he adds, "but pretty, built just for the pleasure and convenience of anyone wanting to eat there." His description continues:

Views of Isfahan: • *The Hezar Jarib garden,* ABOVE, *created by Shah 'Abbas south of the river, by de Bruyn (1718).* • *The Chahar Bagh,* TOP, *as it may have looked in the 17th century, from Flandin and Coste (published in the 1840s).* • *The Mirror Palace (now vanished) in 1856,* OPPOSITE, *in the Sa'adatabad garden, showing its affinity to the Chehel Sotun, from Coste's* Monuments modernes de la Perse.

> Between these most beautiful pavilions there are very large fish ponds in various extravagant forms ... the water coming right up to the paving of the road, leaving ample space at the sides for one to pass on horse or foot. These ponds create a big stream of water which runs in the middle down the length of the avenue in a stone-built channel ... from many of the ponds jets of water spurt up into the air; and in others there are waterfalls producing such beautiful cascades that nothing prettier could be seen.

More than fifty years later, Chardin thought the boulevard one of "the most beautiful I have seen or ever heard of."

113

TRIUMPHANT
GARDENS

The Chahar Bagh continued across the thirty-three-arched Allahverdi Khan Bridge on the road to Shiraz and led to the vast garden or fruit forest of Hezar Jarib, built on the slopes just over the river. Circled with a high wall, "3 miles in compass," it was "a garden deservedly famous," "for beauty contend[ing] with all other in Asia," wrote Thomas Herbert. "You go by Chahar Bagh an even street two miles long a great part of the way being garden walls ... all along planted with broad spreading *chenars* (plane trees), which besides shade serve for use and ornament." In the middle of the 17th century Shah 'Abbas II extended the garden. By Chardin's time, lying on a natural gradient, it was composed of twelve terraces, each one rising a yard or so, and twelve avenues in line with the Chahar Bagh itself and three east-west transverse avenues. Stone-lined water channels, opening out Pasargadae-style into square water basins, ran along every fourth avenue. The garden had 500 water jets, fed by lead pipes. The Palace of Bagh-e Jahan Nama (Garden that Displays the World) was built at the top, from where both river and city were visible. Pavilions and pigeon houses marked corners and the intersection of the walkways and water channels. Chardin was charmed by the murmuring streams, the fragrant flowers, and the bird song in the branches, an incredible "mingling of the senses...

When the waters play in this delightful garden, which often happens, one could see nothing more grand or marvellous, especially in Spring in the season of early flowers, because this garden is covered with them, particularly along the canal and around the basins." The garden still existed when visited by archaeologist Jane Dieulafoy in the 1880s, but today no trace remains among new building developments.

LATER SAFAVID GARDENS
IN ISFAHAN

Chardin was an acute and critical observer who, while acknowledging the success of a disciplined government, deplored the arbitrariness of total royal power. His first visit to Persia was during the reign of Shah 'Abbas II, an expert calligrapher, for whom he made some jewelry. Chardin wrote that Isfahan had 162 mosques, 48 *madraseh*, 1,802 caravanserais, and 273 public baths. His detailed account, almost a gazetteer, of the wonders of Isfahan, includes the Sa'adatabad (Abode of Felicity), on the north bank of the river extending as far as the Khaju Bridge, which Shah 'Abbas

II had constructed in about 1650. Like Hezar Jarib, Sa'adatabad was a haven where the king could relax among the flowers, arbors, and splashing fountains. A 17th-century poet wrote verses about the Sa'adatabad gardens in which he praised the billowing fruit blossom and mauve-flowered Judas trees, scented narcissus, violets, hyacinths, sweet sultan, poppy, anemone, larkspur, iris, tulips, white and gold lilies, damask and musk roses with red and yellow petals, white jasmine, sweet basil, marigolds, hollyhocks, and *Mirabilis jalapa* and tuberoses, already introduced from the New World by the Spanish. A contemporary list of cultivated flowers is long, naming many possibilities.

Chardin returned to Persia in 1673, staying for four and half years. As well as seeing gardens which had matured, he described the pavilion of the Hasht Behesht (Eight Paradises), which stood in the center of the Bagh-e Bolbol (Garden of Nightingales), soon after its completion in 1669. He also watched the signs of decadence emerging—in Shiraz as well as Isfahan—as the irresolute Shah Soleiman (1666–94) failed to fulfil his political and imperial role.

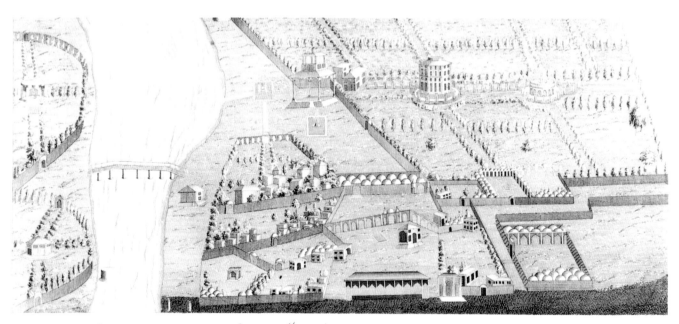

Palais nommé Se'ädet äbäd سعادت آباد *Séjour de la Félicité* Gravé d'après une Peinture Persane

• *The Pol-e Khaju*, ABOVE, *was constructed by Shah ʿAbbas II as both a bridge and a weir. Resting on twenty-four piers, it is divided by narrow channels of rushing water (in spring), each division covered with a pointed arch, above which an arcade of smaller arches runs the length of the bridge. Sluice gates block the channels when water is required upstream. Hexagonal pavilions in the center and at either end of the bridge add architectural significance and provide viewpoints. Steps on the downstream side provide access for washing.* • *Chardin, unable to introduce his engraver, Grelot, into the garden, included a Persian drawing in his* Voyages en Perse *to indicate the size and complexity of the Saʿadatabad,* OPPOSITE, *beside the Zayandeh Rud. The garden had pavilions, kiosks, octagonal lodges, arbors, and terraces and, "When water plays in this pleasant place," he wrote, "it can be imagined as an enchanting site. Fountains are seen all around as far as the eye can see."*

Hasht Behesht

Designed for an open space, the airy pavilion of Hasht Behesht was built under Shah Soleiman in about 1670 as part of the Bagh-e Bolbol. Building and garden reflected the Timurid fashion for outdoor living—as a reception area for courtly entertainments. The octagonal pavilion, with four octagonal rooms on two levels, surrounded an octagonal space covered by a dome, allowing a free flow of movement with the surrounding garden. Delicate floral frescoes decorated the inner walls and the ceilings had a magnificent painted *moqarnas* vault.

To Chardin the Hasht Behesht was an ornamental masterpiece of colorful extravagance and decorative indulgence, appealing to the superficial luxury characteristic of the contemporary court, and a symbol of the decadence of the ruling monarch.

The central pool, decorated with spouting fountains, was fed by a waterway around the pavilion, described by the Westphalian physician and botanist Engelbert Kaempfer in 1685:

The pavilion was located in the middle of a courtyard covered with square pavers. A waterway ran around it, and marble benches were placed at equal distances. Two north-south avenues planted with plane trees led to the pavilion, while water ran in east-west channels to a basin filled with swans and ducks.

◆ *The octagonal pavilion,* RIGHT, *built by Shah Soleiman but renovated in the 19th and 20th centuries, overlooks a water tank with fountains to cool the air. Today, pine trees shade both sides of the building. In the 17th century, the garden was an open reception area for courtly entertainments within the Bagh-e Bolbol, off the Chahar Bagh.* ◆ *Plane trees and elms* (Ulmus minor), ABOVE, *line the lateral avenues.*

PALACES ON THE CASPIAN

Shah 'Abbas and his peripatetic court spent winters in the warmer climate on the Caspian coast, traveling north in a great cavalcade and using the smaller utilitarian "lodges" and caravanserais he had had built along the way. He usually stayed in the province of Mazanderan, his mother's birthplace, until after the *Nou Ruz* in March. The sea to the north and the slopes of the wild mountains of the Alborz to the south afforded the Shah some protection from his enemies, besides enabling him to avoid the winters of extreme cold on the high Iranian plateau. Perhaps he was also drawn there by the beauties of nature extolled by Ferdousi:

> *Mazanderan is the bower of spring . . .*
> *Tulips and hyacinths abound*
> *On every lawn; and all around*
> *Blooms like a garden in its prime,*
> *Fostered by that delicious clime*
> *The nightingale sits on every spray*
> *And pours his soft melodious lay:*
> *Each rural spot its sweets discloses:*
> *Each streamlet is the dew of roses. . .*

Shah 'Abbas built a set of royal palaces and gardens (at least six palaces and hunting lodges) in Mazanderan, settings for the court and for his harem, where he received travelers such as Pietro della Valle and foreign ambassadors including Sir Dodmore Cotton and Thomas Herbert. He also introduced many new people to the area from regions he had sacked and looted: from Georgia, Armenia, and other Ottoman lands, moving Christians, Jews, and Muslims, exploiting their energy and skills to develop and farm the fertile land. Around Tahan on the Caspian which he renamed Farahabad, meaning the "joyful colony" from Arab *farah* (joy) and Persian *abad* (settlement), he encouraged the silk industry by planting innumerable mulberry trees.

With no winter frosts and annual rainfall of as much as 57 inches, the land was a jungle with malarial marshes in much of the plain lying along the shore—sometimes only a few miles wide but elsewhere stretching 30 miles from the sea to the foot of the wooded mountains, a completely different vegetation from that found on the arid plateau. The climate and topography of the Caspian coast could have allowed a style of garden to develop that was different from the balanced symmetry of the traditional layout, but the formula remained much as it was in Isfahan—a series of interconnected gardens, palaces, and pavilions. The buildings in the gardens, as at Isfahan, were located at the end of a long pool or in the center of the garden where water channels met, resembling jewels in elaborate settings. What was new about the Caspian gardens was the availability of water, which at Ashraf enabled 'Abbas to build terraced gardens on steeply sloping ground with rushing water cascades. While the layout and function of the garden remained the same, it became an ordered oasis in the midst of a richly fertile verdant plain where reptiles lurked in the swamps. Wolves, bears, and tigers roamed in the steep forested terrain of the foothills above. Nature, in the shape of wild animals and jungle vegetation, was still the enemy, although heat and thirst were not to be feared.

Shah 'Abbas began building his principal summer retreats on the level plains of Mazanderan in 1611. Farahabad, near the coast on the banks of the River Tajand, became a large town during his reign, but it was destroyed by Cossacks from the Don in 1668, leaving nothing to be seen today. A paved causeway above the level of the flooded ground connected the palace complex to Ashraf, 5 miles inland to the east, at the foot of wooded mountains.

In his *Travels and Adventures in the Persian Provinces on the Southern Banks of the Caspian Sea*, published in 1826, James B. Fraser's account of Farahabad indicates that Shah 'Abbas

◆ *The public garden in Behshahr, in the foothills of the north face of the Alborz Mountains, is all that remains of the Ashraf garden of Shah 'Abbas. It retains the traditional* chahar bagh *layout, water cascades down a narrow waterway, and terraces extend as orchards to either side.*

created a version of the *maidan* complex at Isfahan but on a smaller scale, the open square measuring only 200 by 100 paces, its axis from north to south. At the northern end, almost on the shore, a walled enclosure was further divided to provide an area for public receptions and court functions and a private garden for the ruler, a pattern repeated in many of the constructions. The private palace overlooking the sea was called the Jahan Nama (View of the World). The square itself was surrounded by arcades like a vast caravanserai, with a mosque to the south.

Sir Dodmore Cotton and Thomas Herbert visited Farahabad in 1628. Arriving without presents, the English were hardly welcome, although Cotton congratulated the Shah on beating the Turks and the delegation secured 10,000 bales of silk each year for the King of England. They followed the Shah to Qazvin where Cotton was to die from dysentery and exhaustion, leaving Herbert to return to the Gulf via Qum, Kashan, Isfahan, and Shiraz. Herbert found the palace at Farahabad luxurious with a "curious summer house, excelling all his other for prospect, painting, hammam, waterworks and a forest which is stored with game of all sorts." With rare attention to detail, he describes the elaborate garden as having two large courts, with a series of beds for spring bulbs and summer flowers "formed into grass plots and knots of various sort, replenished with variety of trees and flowers, which makes the place exceeding pleasant; amongst others tulips and roses were there so plentiful." Spreading plane trees, maples (*Acer velutinum*), and chestnuts surrounded "the place with so much beauty." Both black and white mulberries (the leaves of the latter the food of silk worms) produced their fruit in July. "The rooms of the palace were adorned with looking glasses, with Muscovinan glass windows cemented with gold or what resembled it." The great recorder Chardin also visited Farahabad but he was so interested in the palace treasures—dishes and basins of "porcelain and China, Agate, Coral, Ambar, Rock Crystal" and a Jasper fountain covered with gold—that he omitted to describe the gardens.

Pietro della Valle arrived at Farahabad in February 1618, but had to wait until May before being summoned to kiss the Emperor's hand at Ashraf, a day's journey distant, where, at a feast, he was made to drink wine which he detested. The Emperor appeared with his turban on back to front to amuse his guests. At Ashraf della Valle found the city built in a wooded area used for hunting, with countless inhabitants but little of interest except the royal house, still not finished. The gardens of the Chehel Sotun on the level ground at the foot of the hills were still being planted and pavilions and loggias were under construction on the lower slopes. Shady avenues with a central water channel led through a courtyard to the end of the garden and the Divan Khaneh (Audience Chamber), its walls and floor covered with beautiful carpets.

Later della Valle, accompanied by the Vizier of Mazanderan, was able to visit the women's residence, where the walled Bagh-e Tappeh (Garden of Little Hills) was filled with orange and lemon trees and fragrant flowers.

 • *A native maple* (Acer velutinum), ABOVE, *from the Caspian forests.* • *The hilltop palace,* OPPOSITE, *overlooking the Caspian at Behshahr, was restored in the 20th century by Reza Shah Pahlavi to resemble an Italian villa. According to Byron, the villa was small, "its tilework coarse," but the garden was "more romantic."*

Herbert's description of 'Abbas's Bagh-e Shah at Ashraf is more detailed, making it possible to reconstruct the layout of the gardens. A public garden in the town (now Behshahr) is all that remains of the splendid complex built by 'Abbas. Originally there was a series of eight palaces connected by *chahar bagh* enclosures on different levels, with central water cascades fed by mountain springs, each with its own pavilion and *divan khaneh*. At least one was the private palace of the Shah and another, the Bagh-e Haram, was reserved for the harem. A villa perched on a hill a few miles to the west gave views to the sea.

The Bagh-e Saheb-Zaman was the most southerly of the gardens in the Ashraf complex and was almost certainly where the reception of guests took place, if not in the Chehel Sotun nearer the entrance. From the terraces it was possible to feel the mountain breezes and see the Caspian Sea. Herbert's account of a pavilion continues: "the ground chambers were large, quadrangular, archt, and richly gilded above and on their sides…below spread most valuable Carpets of silk and gold; in the centre were Tancks full of crystaline water." Sparkling fountains had basins of rare marbles inlaid with precious stones, while treasures of gems and costly containers were everywhere on display adding to an *Arabian Nights'* fantasy. Bagh-e Cheshmeh (Garden of the Spring), had a series of stepped terraces and the pavilion was crowned with a dome as recorded by an 18th-century traveler, Jonas Hanway, who described the views, the superlative mountain backdrop, and the pleasing thoughts inspired by the murmur of numerous cascades and the music of birds. After the death of 'Abbas in 1629 (at either Farahabad or Ashraf), Ashraf was overrun by Turkomans and went into swift decline until partly rescued by Nader Shah in the following century, and Mohammad Shah, an early Qajar ruler, also attempted repairs.

When Robert Byron visited Ashraf in the 1930s two gardens where Shah 'Abbas had received Sir Dodmore Cotton in 1627 and the palace on the hill were all that survived of the "royal pleasaunce." He gives this account of the gardens in *The Road to Oxiana*:

Long stone waterways proceed through gently sloping meadows, negotiating each fall in level with a flat stone glissade in the Mogul style. Whether this style originated in Persia, India or Oxiana, it is proper to a barren landscape only. Here framed in grass and bracken, it becomes slightly excessive, as an Italian garden is in Ireland … the other garden illustrates the same scale of ideas as Shah 'Abbas put into effect at Isfahan. From the hill at the back, where pink orchids were flowering in the undergrowth, a cypress avenue descends through a walled enclosure of several acres, which is dotted with other cypresses in the manner of an English park. The waterway runs inside the avenue, and like that of the Villa Lante, passes between two pavilions, that are joined by a roofed arcade that acts as a bridge … the square pools, now dry, which used to receive each water-glissade, [has] copings carved with holes for fairy lights in the form of wicks floating on oil.

7 Gardens of rulers and merchants

"The long slope of the garden, from end to end, was a dazzling glancing stream of water, broken up by dashing cascades and adorned with fountains rising high into the air." Ella Sykes *Persia and its People* 1910

 GARDENS CREATED IN THE 18TH AND 19TH CENTURIES STILL EVOKED AN IMAGE OF PARADISE, although their sacred meaning was, perhaps, less important than their role as symbols of power and prestige. For the believer, Paradise was a promise for the future; to the non-believer the enclosed garden provided architectural order and protection, to be interpreted as a metaphor for the well-managed kingdom.

Fed by mountain springs and natural streams, many of the garden sites in the old cities had ancient origins, those we see today representing layers of history, added to and altered through the centuries as a result of conquests, floods, and earthquakes. We know from poems by Sa'di and Hafez that gardens existed in medieval Shiraz—indeed many may have existed before the time of the great poets. So while the 18th-century pleasure parks often have pavilions that date to the later Qajar period, and the stonework, tiling, and mosaics may be comparatively recent, the gardens are based on the immemorial Persian outline, that of an almost canonical *chahar bagh*. Each walled-in space is composed of a long axis, crossed by one or several cross perpendiculars which inter-sect to create four quadrants for planting. The main axis is a water channel lined with walkways, with flowerbeds at a lower level. In most cases, the garden pavilion is placed at the top of a slope with water before it opening into a wide pool before narrowing to descend the slope as a channel.

Many gardens created in the 20th century pay similar homage to the classic Persian garden.

Shiraz, city of roses and nightingales, cypresses and wine, poetry and painted miniatures, has been one of the most important cultural sites in Persia since medieval times, renowned for its artists and scholars. An oasis to the desert traveler and with a perfect climate, the town is situated in a valley at the bottom of the pass from Isfahan. No wonder that the traveler cresting the ridge, as he approached the gateway housing a Koran, after long hard days in the desert felt he had come to a paradise "which turns the heart of the wanderer from his native land." He could look down, as you can today, on the blue-tiled domes sparkling in the sunlight, embowered in greenery lying between pink-tinged mountain ranges.

Set in a well-watered and wonderfully fertile plain famous for its grapes and wine, Shiraz has long been associated with gardens. Above all it was the birthplace of the two most beloved Persian poets, Sa'di and Hafez. Ibn Battuta, who could have met Hafez on his second visit in July 1347, praised it as second only to Damascus in the beauty of its bazaars, fruit gardens, and rivers. He admired especially the stream known as Roknabad, celebrated by Hafez, the "water of which is very sweet, very cold in summer and warm in winter, and gushes out of a fountain on the lower slope of a hill." During the reign of Shah 'Abbas the city benefited from the administration of the governor of Fars, Emam Qoli Khan, who, inspired by improvements in Isfahan, laid out a wide Chahar Bagh central avenue flanked by pavilions, palaces, gardens, and *madrasehs*. When Thomas Herbert saw it in 1628 as he passed through Shiraz on the way to Isfahan to wait on Shah 'Abbas, he found "the earth dry but green; the air salubrious, though sharp a little … and nothing more complained of by the inhabitants than want of water." The gardens were both beautiful and large, some 800 paces long and 400 broad."

Herbert was probably describing the 11th-century terraced garden of Bagh-e Takht (Garden of the Throne) when he wrote:

> The King's garden challenges superiority over all the rest … being square every way 2,000 paces … most of them safeguarded with walls 14 foot high and 4 foot thick; and which from their spaciousness and plenty of trees resemble groves or wildernesses, but by that name—Persian word is *bawt* or *bagh*—they abound in lofty pyramidal cypresses, broad spreading chenars, tough elm, straight ash, knotty pines, fragrant mastics, kingly oaks, sweet myrtles, useful maples; and of fruit trees are grapes … pomegranates, pomecitrons [the citron, *Citrus medica*], oranges, lemons, pistachios, apples, pears, peaches, chestnuts, cherries, quinces, walnut, apricots, plums, almonds, figs, dates and melons of both sorts exceeding fair and of incomparable sweetness; also flowers rare to the eye, sweet to the smell, and useful in physic.

At *Nou Ruz* "the gardens are opened for all to walk in," Herbert added, "the women likewise for fourteen days have liberty to appear in public, and when loose (like birds enfranchised) lose themselves in a labyrinth of wanton sport." On leaving Shiraz, he felt inspired to write an ode to the city's paradise of gardens which ends:

◆ PRECEDING PAGES *The Bagh-e Shahzadeh.* ◆ *A view of 17th-century Shiraz from the Koran Gate on a hill to the north of the town,* ABOVE, *from Chardin's* Voyages en Perse.

*Farewell, sweet place, for, as from thee I went,
my thoughts did run on Adam's banishment.*

The well-traveled Chardin visited Shiraz in 1674 during his second visit to Persia. Floods in 1668 had reduced the number of houses by two-thirds from 12,000 to 4,000 and decimated the population. Shah Safi I (1629–41) had had the viceroy murdered and imposed direct rule by appointed commissioners. Although lamenting the dilapidation of Emam Qoli Khan's palace, where marble-sided ponds and fountains lay under crumbling ceilings decorated with arabesques in silver and gold leaf, Chardin could still appreciate the many gardens with their tree canopies and flowers. High-reaching and broad-standing plane and cypress trees brought shade and comfort. At least twenty public gardens lined the main street which descended from the city gateway. He mentions a royal garden, probably Bagh-e Takht, and the Bagh-e Ferdous (Garden of Paradise), which had a pool "125 paces along one side."

Seven years after an Afghan army invaded Khorasan and captured Isfahan, Shiraz was also sacked, in 1722, and again in 1744 as a reprisal for the rebellion by the province's governor, this time by Nader Shah from Mashad who had set himself on the throne in 1736, deposing 'Abbas III (1732–6), the last of the now ineffective Safavid dynasty. Nader Shah's eleven-year rule was warlike and brutal. With the army living off the land and heavy taxes being levied to support his ceaseless campaigns, the populace suffered. He had no interest in establishing courtly residences and gardens, and made little contribution to Persian culture. His conquests, however, brought the nation considerable prestige, creating an extensive empire. Nader Shah recovered Armenia and Georgia from the Ottomans, drove the Afghans from Khorasan and Herat, and captured Delhi in 1739, returning with fabulous treasures from the Mughal Empire.

After his assassination in 1747, Nader Shah's empire broke up. Karim Khan, the *vakil* (regent) and chief of the Zand tribe, began his reign in 1759 in Fars and made Shiraz his capital, his wise and firm rule extending ultimately to Isfahan and most of southern Iran. He continued in power until his death in 1779, successfully repulsing the Qajars, a Turkish tribe from Mazanderan.

Shiraz fared well under Karim Khan. It was a golden age for the city under a benevolent ruler, who lacked the brutal habits of many previous and future shahs. He stimulated trade links with the Persian Gulf, bringing prosperity to the city's inhabitants, and inaugurated a period of rebuilding. Shiraz was embellished by avenues, palaces, garden pavilions, mosques, and a vaulted bazaar, the Bazar-e Vakil. Many gardens and pavilions that had been damaged in the floods were repaired during this period of peace and plenty, among them the Bagh-e Delgosha (Garden of Heart's Ease), which may date to the Seljuk period, and the Bagh-e Jahan Nama (Garden that Displays the World), reputedly established in the 13th century. Karim Khan Zand laid out the quartered garden and central rectangular pool at Bagh-e Nazar. Its reception hall, a small octagonal building called Kolah Farangi (Foreigner's Hat), was his mausoleum until it was vandalized by the first Qajar, Agha Mohammad Khan.

During the 19th century many Qajars settled in Shiraz and "improved" gardens of much earlier origin which had been damaged by earthquakes in 1823 and 1852. Edward G. Browne visited Shiraz during the spring of 1888, arriving during *Nou Ruz*. Already enraptured by his view from the mountain pass, he dismounted at his host's gate into a "large and handsome courtyard paved with stones and traversed by a little stream of clear water which flowed from a large square tank at the upper end. On either side stood a row of stately sycamores, interspersed with orange-trees, while a mass of beautiful flowers tastefully grouped lent brightness to the view and fragrance to the air." During his stay Browne visited many other gardens in Shiraz, some of which may well still exist behind tall walls. A Persian gazetteer of 1896 lists at least twenty-eight, many named after their owners but others with imaginative and joyful names such as the Gardens of Prospect, of Saffron, of Pomegranates, and of the Falcon.

Bagh-e Eram

With gurgling water channels and lush planting of shade-giving trees and citrus orchards, the Bagh-e Eram (Garden of Heaven), on the northern bank of the River Kushk, takes its name from the fabled garden in Arabia cited in the Koran as "iram [heaven] adorned with pillars." Both pavilion and garden are said to have been built in the middle of the 19th century by the Il-Khan or paramount chief of the Qashqa'i tribe. The garden's layout, however, with a large reflecting pool and four waterways, almost certainly owes its origins to an earlier era and may have been imposed on an 18th-century garden called Bagh-e Shah, established in the Seljuk period and described by travelers, such as Cornelius de Bruyn.

The fine pavilion, facing south down the long axis, was designed by a local architect, Haji Mohammad Hasan. Thirty rooms on two stories were decorated with tiles on which were poems by Hafez. The pool and the watercourse, descending in terraces, were built on a massive scale.

Sir Denis Wright, British ambassador to Iran in October 1965, was present at a dinner given there for Princess Alexandra and Angus Ogilvy by Asadullah Alam, former Prime Minister and at the time Chancellor of Shiraz University and the Shah's closest friend. It was "a lavish and beautifully done party at Bagh-e Eram— a sit-down dinner followed by Qashqa'i women in their best, dancing in the garden, and a famous singer from Tehran."

◆ *The Qajar pavilion, LEFT, at the top of the garden, looks out over the wide reflecting pool and the lower garden, where axial watercourses, orange groves, and cypresses confirm its Persian origins.* ◆ *Water from a spring behind the pavilion flows through the building to the pool, OPPOSITE, and feeds the central water axis which descends to the cypress alley. Palms and Judas trees (also illustrated on page 36), lilacs and exotics create a luxuriant garden wilderness.* ◆ *Modern roses, ABOVE, with a long flowering period, and nightingales singing in the trees, continue the city of Shiraz's association with poetry and gardens.*

0 5 10 20   40 metres
0 25 50   100   feet

♦ *The plan of the Bagh-e Eram,* ABOVE, *shows the axial watercourses and ordered geometry of an extended* chahar bagh. *Lateral sunken beds are planted with spring-flowering fruit trees, as they have been since the first Persian gardens evolved.* ♦ *Quiet planting between cypress alleys and orange groves,* LEFT, *accentuates the "bones" of the layout.* ♦ *Marigolds, stocks, and irises in the upper garden,* OPPOSITE, *demonstrate the skill of the gardeners in what is now Shiraz's University Botanic Garden. Whereas the earliest Persian gardens relied on spring bulbs for color, there being few summer-flowering plants, annual and perennial exotics are available today. Four o'clocks* (Mirabilis jalapa), *tobacco plants* (Nicotiana), *salvias, and zinnias from the New World all thrive in Shiraz.*

Naranjestan

The town house of Qavam al-Mulk, hereditary head of the Khamseh tribal federation, is known as the Naranjestan for the orange trees flanking the walkways between the *biruni* and the *talar*. Built by the Qavam-Shirazi family in 1870, in the reign of Naser ad-Din Shah, the Naranjestan typifies the elegance and refinement enjoyed by upper-class Persians in enclosed dwellings.

The main rooms of the *biruni* (offices for business and entertainment) at the entrance faced east along the garden toward the *talar* (reception hall), where the Qavam al-Mulk received male visitors. Decorated with mirror work, and with windows of colored glass (from Russia) in typical Qajar style, the opulent *talar* looked over the elaborately patterned garden, the rills and pools lying between flowerbeds filled with roses and perennials. An avenue of tall date palms, flanked by the orange trees, provided shade. Women were segregated in the *haram* (sanctuary).

♦ *From the* biruni, *the garden stretches east toward the* talar, ABOVE, *in a series of elliptical pools, linked by a narrow rill, between beds of massed annuals. Orange trees lining the paths are backed by towering date palms.* ♦ *The view from the* talar, OPPOSITE, *is framed by columns supporting a ceiling decorated with mosaic mirror work.* ♦ *Interior walls and ceilings,* TOP LEFT, *catch the light reflected in the large basin that feeds the water channel running down the center of the garden. At night chandeliers sustain the jewel-like effect.* ♦ *The recess in the center of the* biruni *is decorated with tiles,* TOP RIGHT, *depicting servants carrying drinks and dishes of food beneath a flower frieze.*

Bagh-e Golshan

Karim Khan's reign, besides insuring good government throughout Fars, also covered the making of one of the most enduringly beautiful *chahar bagh* gardens in Persia, that of Bagh-e Golshan in Tabas, established in the 1760s by Amir Hasan Khan who moved the oasis and palm-tree groves further south from their original site. Until 1978 the garden was owned by Amir 'Ali Khan Sheibany.

The oasis at Tabas stands in the *garmsir* at only 2,000 feet above sea level on the Iranian plateau between the Dasht-e Kavir and the Dasht-e Lut. The town does not depend on *qanats* for its ample water supply—in spring the water rills of Bagh-e Golshan are rushing brown torrents—but on a stream, fed by natural springs which lie in the low foothills, which never fails in spite of evaporation in the summer heat.

Sven Hedin, the Swedish explorer, stayed in Tabas in 1886 on his way from India, describing it with high praise.

"Nothing can be more charming than an oasis in the desert, no oasis can be more beautiful than Tebbes [Tabas]" with the snow-clad humps of the Kuh-i Shotori (Camel Hill) rising above the desert in the distance. Having crossed the salt desert, with its "white surface quivering in the dazzling light to look like water" and listened to jackals howling at night, on his arrival at Tabas Hedin passed an ancient two-trunked tamarisk tree, where the "murmur of running brooks is the most delightful music" between rows of mulberry trees, weeping willows, and orange groves. He saw fruit and vegetables growing in the area, besides tobacco, an essential part of Tabas wealth. He also noted the deadly snakes and scorpions and the swift-footed hairy spiders which could keep up with a galloping horse.

In the 20-acre garden, laid out on a slope, Hedin noted the two canals that converged into a tank, above which the date palms stood out in dark outline; their "harsh parchment-like leaves," he wrote, "rustle and rattle as the desert

wind whistles through them."

Until the 1970s the governor's house faced the garden gates but earthquakes obliterated the building, besides most of the rest of the houses, an old mosque, and the windtowers for which the town was renowned. The entrance building was aligned with the central watercourse and its rushing cascades opened out to a wide pool. Clipped hedges separated sixteen garden plots on the terraces. Today, pomegranates, jasmine, acacia, almonds, citrus, cycads, and fruiting palm trees are underplanted with roses and spring stocks, a testimony to the fertile soil and mild winters, and the skills of the local gardeners. Dark cypress trees, dating to the garden's inception, alternate with the soft gray leaves of the Euphratic poplar (*Populus euphratica*) and with groves of eucalyptus from Australia. Spreading pines provide welcome shade for modern roses, hollyhocks, and other perennials growing in the formal flowerbeds which flank the channels and pool, with orchards to the side where nightingales sing.

♦ The plan, OPPOSITE, shows the garden's four-fold layout, each quadrant to either side of the watercourse and main transverse walkway further divided in four. ♦ The elevation, ABOVE, shows the levels through which water descends in parallel channels that widen and narrow again in front of the pavilion. ♦ Richly planted flowerbeds, OPPOSITE ABOVE, between the water channels near the entrance to the garden are testament to plentiful and unfailing water, and industrious gardeners. ♦ The photograph of the pavilion, OPPOSITE BELOW RIGHT, was taken by Sir Denis Wright in 1965 before its destruction in the earthquake. The pelican is one of a pair which lived in the garden.

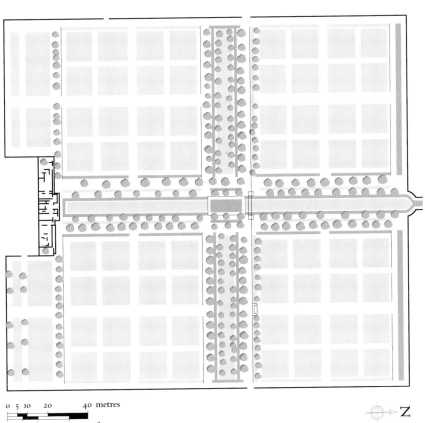

0 5 10   20   40 metres

0   25   50   100   feet

N

Bagh-e Shahzadeh

Surrounded by stony desert, with the great Dasht-e Lut to the east, and backed to north and south by distant mountains, snow-capped even in summer, the beautiful Bagh-e Shahzadeh (Prince's Garden or Garden of Farman Farma), near the shrine of Ne'matollah Vali at Mahan, expresses the spirit of a true oasis garden. It was built in the early 1880s by Naser ad-Douleh, a governor of Kerman (1880–91)

and the elder brother of Farman Farma, a powerful Qajar prince.

Water from the mountains to the south is stored in a vast cistern outside the walls to feed pools, cascades, and fountains. The summer pavilion has a view up the terraced waterway, flanked by flowerbeds, overhung with tall dark cypresses and airy willows. On either side, at every level, compartments stretch out toward the perimeter walls, containing orchards of pears and pomegranates. At the top of

the garden, glimpsed through a curtain of water jets, was the governor's residence.

Within a few years of its construction, Ella Sykes, sister of Percy Sykes, British consul in Kerman from 1895 to 1905, described the garden's long slope, with a "dazzling glancing stream of water, broken up by dashing cascades and adorned with fountains rising high into the air, while the August sun, gleaming on their foam, tinted them with all the colours of the rainbow."

◆ *Cypresses and willows frame a view down the terraced waterway to the ruined summer pavilion,* OPPOSITE, *at the southern entrance to the garden. Water cascading down the steep gradient pauses in rectangular pools, where its reflections create a sense of space under the enclosing dark trees.* ◆ *Massive walls,* LEFT, *providing protection from desert wind and dust, are one of the garden's traditional Persian elements.* ◆ *A stream,* BELOW, *runs through the orchards that stretch out to the perimeter walls.*

◆ *The plan of Bagh-e Shahzadeh,* RIGHT, *shows the extended* chahar bagh *pattern within the walled enclosure, the governor's house at the top of the slope, the central waterway with lateral compartments on each level, and the summer pavilion at the entrance.* ◆ *A view up the garden from the summer pavilion,* OPPOSITE, *shows the steps and terraces built to adjust the levels.* ◆ *The large pool,* BOTTOM, *on the second level by the summer pavilion.* ◆ *Vines,* BELOW, *receive ample water from irrigation channels. Cultivation is by the traditional mattock.*

N

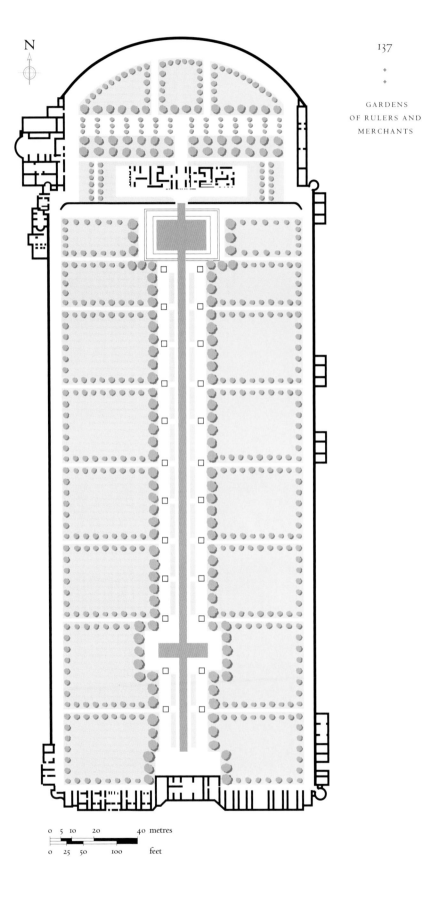

0 5 10   20   40 metres

0   25   50   100   feet

Tehran has been a capital city for only two centuries. Until the 16th century when Shah Tahmasp surrounded it with walls and towers, it was hardly more than a village midway between Qazvin and Isfahan, dependent on *qanats* for its water supply. Shah 'Abbas built a garden there which Pietro della Valle visited in 1618, observing that two-thirds of the land inside the walls was orchards and gardens. Karim Khan used the *arg* (citadel) as his military headquarters. Tehran became the capital under the first Qajar shah, Agha Mohammad Khan, who was finally crowned there in 1796, having brought the whole country under his authority after the death of Karim Khan in 1779. He had defeated the remaining member of the Zand dynasty at Kerman, killing him by torture and putting out the eyes of 20,000 of the town's inhabitants. A year later this cruel tyrant was assassinated. The reign of his nephew, Fath 'Ali Shah (1797–1834), ushered in a century of relative peace, dominated by British and Russian rivalry over political and commercial interests.

Fath 'Ali Shah was a cultivated and extravagant ruler who initiated much building and restoration work in Tehran and elsewhere in Persia. He transformed the *arg* by adding a *maidan*, private royal apartments, a *haramsarai* (harem), and administrative buildings. In 1806 he completed the Golestan (Rose Palace), with a *divan khaneh* (audience hall) and a large square garden with a rectangular pool, lined with plane

• *The Divan Khaneh,* ABOVE, *of the Golestan (Rose Palace) in Tehran was completed by Fath 'Ali Shah in 1806 as part of his reconstruction of the citadel. The engraving, from Flandin and Coste's* Voyage en Perse 1840–1842, *gives an impression of the ornate façade and shows the large canvas hangings that were rolled down for shade.* • *Fallen pillars,* OPPOSITE, *are all that remain of the steps and water cascades in the 19th-century Bagh-e Malek below Golabdarreh on the mountain slopes above Tehran.*

trees. For receptions carpeted tents were erected on the green lawns, bright with tulips and narcissi, anemones and poppies. Sir Robert Ker Porter attended one of the glittering receptions held around the pool soon after the garden was made. He described Fath 'Ali Shah appearing in a blaze of dazzling jewels, a lofty tiara of three elevations on his head, and taking his place on the white marble throne in the *talar*. In the last decade of the 19th century, Lord Curzon attended a royal levée given by Naser ad-Din Shah and described the garden as "divided by paved avenues and gravel paths, with flowerbeds, tanks and extensive lakes" with little iron bridges crossing the numerous channels often lined with blue tiles, the pools alive with fishes and "decked with swans and water fowl."

Many of the 18th- and 19th-century gardens in Tehran were built by rulers and Persian nobles on the cool and breezy slopes of the Alborz to the north of the city, an area now swallowed up by suburbs, its water supply provided by *qanats* from the mountain springs. Just as the Mughal emperors found sanctuary in the Kashmir foothills from the dust and heat of the northern plains of India, so the Qajar dynasty sought refuge from the blistering Tehran summers in the mountain air. The first Qajar, Agha Mohammad Khan, built a summer resort in Shemiran, 1,200 feet above

the city, which he called Mohammadieh. In contrast to the capital in the plain below, the shady well-watered site afforded his court, at first accommodated in tented camps, a welcome escape from oppressive heat. Fath 'Ali Shah built summer retreats at Cheshmeh-e 'Ali near his birthplace at Damghan (see Chapter 2), the Qasr-e Qajar (Castle of the Qajars), and the Negarestan Palace, to the east of Tehran and outside the original walls.

The Negarestan, meaning the Picture Gallery, completed in 1810 and set in about 10 acres, was Fath 'Ali Shah's favorite residence. It took its name from the Divan Khaneh, an almost circular building where he displayed portraits of all the shahs and also of staff of the French and English legations, including Sir John Malcolm, an early-19th-century envoy at the Persian court. The garden was centered on a large pool and fountain set within an octagonal pavilion, the Kolah Farangi (Foreigner's Hat). Nightingales sang in the trees, which were underplanted with roses, lilacs, and other

fragrant shrubs. This may have been the garden that inspired the poet laureate Saba (Fath 'Ali Khan) to write a eulogy about the legendary garden of Eram, which demonstrates garden fashions of the period and shows how a poet had to placate and flatter his patron. Edward G. Browne in *A Year Amongst the Persians* (1887–8) describes a marble bath furnished with a long smooth *glissoire*, called by the Persians *sursurak*, down which the numerous ladies of the harem used to slide.

Later shahs built summer palaces in the environs of Tehran—elegant quarters for their wives and families, such as Sahebqaranieh, a palace of Naser ad-Din Shah, during whose reign (1848–96) the government of British India declared war on Iran following the Persian capture of Herat; later Britain and Russia gained various concessions over Iran's natural resources. Sahebqaranieh had a commanding position on a steeply sloping site at Niavaran, affording a superb view of the city lying in the plain. The

⬩ *Engravings from Flandin and Coste's* Voyage en Perse 1840–1842 *of Fath 'Ali Shah's Qasr-e Qajar, built in the early 19th century on a hill 2½ miles outside Tehran. The complex rivaled in splendor all other contemporary royal dwellings, its garden constructed on descending terraces,* ABOVE, *to a vast water tank on the plain below.* ⬩ *An interior courtyard of the Qasr-e Qajar,* OPPOSITE, *with reflecting pool and trees for shade, shows the pavilion from which the Shah looked down to the garden and the city spread out below.*

garden descended in a series of terraces with tile-lined water channels and included formal elements that were more foreign-inspired than Persian. It was enlarged in the 1930s by Reza Shah Pahlavi (1925–40). The palace at Sa'dabad, set in a 40-acre park a few miles from Niavaran, was also built in the Qajar period. Nearby villages, such as Vanak and Evin, contained more royal gardens, as well as some belonging to rich Persians, such as the Bagh-e Mostoufi, laid out in the 1930s and still beautiful with rills and cascades. The Bagh-e Malek below Golabdarreh on the slopes above the River Darband may date to the time of Nader Shah, but most of the steps, pillars, and water features were constructed much more recently. A few fallen columns, rills, and stone stairways remain, hidden among undergrowth. In the 20th century mountain districts, such as Shemiran, Tajrish, and Niavaran, at first almost camping sites, were developed as refuges from summer's heat in the city. There the better-off built simple summer cabins and elegant villas with elaborate terraced gardens and cascades, made possible by the ample water supply. Other gardens were laid out in the hills above Tehran by European traders or for summer residences for foreign ambassadors. The Italian ambassador's Persian-style garden at Farmanieh has flowerbeds flanked by tall plane trees.

The last royal palace of the Qajars was the Qasr-e Farahabad (Castle of the Abode of Joy), built a few miles east of Tehran on the orders of Muzaffar ad-Din Shah, who succeeded in 1896 after the assassination of his father, Naser ad-Din Shah. A weak and extravagant sovereign who showed no aptitude for affairs of state, Muzaffar allowed nobles and landlords to amass fortunes, whereas the ordinary people were highly taxed and public officials did not receive salaries. The Shah bankrupted the treasury with expensive trips to Europe and, according to one report, modeled the glaring white palace at Qasr-e Farahabad on the Trocadero in Paris. Set in a garden of about 50 acres outside the city walls, it overlooked terraces and cascades to a vast lake.

Bagh-e Mostoufi

The Mostoufi Garden near the village of Vanak on the slopes above Tehran was laid out within an enclosing wall during the 1930s. With ample water from the mountains, there was plenty of scope for developing water features—large pools, cascades, fountains, and rills—which reflect the Persian ideal.

From dark square water tanks at the top of the garden, a rill gurgles over steps into a smaller rectangular pool set with low bubbling fountains. A further rill exits to an octagonal fountain from which water travels to the pavilion, where in the shade of tall plane trees, a narrow channel edged in box reaches its final destination

before escaping into the wood below. The low house, sited to the side of the complex at the bottom of the slope, was made with modern cement, its proportions in perfect sympathy with the water features.

Surrounded by tall trees that are mirrored in the upper pool, fruit trees and shrubs are reminders of the garden's beauty. Lilacs, wild cherries, walnut trees, and old plane trees are mixed with viburnums and forsythias. Ivy and periwinkle carpet the ground under the trees. In more open areas the small blue-flowered ixiolirion, roses, and pomegranates thrive next to a pergola draped with a yellow Banksian rose. The complex included fruit orchards and vegetable sections above the main garden.

The rectangular pool, ABOVE LEFT, *on the garden's upper level.* ◆ *Ixiolirion tartaricum,* ABOVE RIGHT, *has seeded in the garden, the hot dry summers providing the conditions needed for the bulbs to ripen.* ◆ *Water from the octagonal fountain emerges in a water rill,* RIGHT, *edged with box and shaded by plane trees. A Banksian rose flowers in a glade where the garden spreads out to either side of the central water feature.*

THE BRITISH LEGATION
IN TEHRAN

The first British Legation or Mission House was built between 1812 and 1813 by Sir Gore Ouseley, the first British ambassador to be appointed to the Qajar court. It was also the first foreign mission permitted to have a permanent residence in Persia. It remained the principal residence of the Legation for some sixty years, although from the 1830s onward, Gulhak, 6 miles away on the slopes north of Tehran, became a summer retreat, first in tents, then in houses. Twice a year furniture, bedding, and chinaware were moved between Tehran and Gulhak.

Situated due south of the main bazaar in Tehran, the building, seen across a courtyard garden, had an imposing classical façade, 40 feet across, with four Doric columns supporting a frieze and cornice. Wide shallow steps at the center led up to a verandah paved with colored tiles. The small garden in front of the building was in English style with formal flowerbeds and paved walks, while the large garden across the street had a traditional Persian layout, with double rows of cypresses crossing at right angles at the center and an orchard of pomegranates and plane trees underplanted with vegetables and melons.

Lady Sheil arrived as wife of the British minister in 1849 and quickly realized that "Gardening in Persia is not an easy matter to bring to perfection. First," she explained, "there is the difficulty of making the gardeners do as they are told, and then twice a week the garden is flooded and the beds drowned … the power of the sun in summer is so intense that flowers blow and wither in a day." Fortunately, Lady Sheil was able to "borrow" the Shah's English gardener Mr Burton who, having been engaged at the request of the late Mohammad Shah (d. 1848), was somewhat at a loose end as the young Naser ad-Din Shah showed no interest in his work. Lady Sheil describes the mission garden as:

> but a melancholy place of recreation; lugubrious rows of cypresses, the emblem of the churchyard in the

east, crossed each other at right angles, and to complete the picture, the deserted, neglected, little tombs of the children of former Ministers occupied a prominent place, and filled one sometimes with gloomy forebodings.

Nevertheless, she was able to astonish everyone with the excellence of her celery and cauliflowers—vegetables occupying her mind more than flowers. The mission gardeners, as Gertrude Bell found later at the new legation, were always industrious *guebres*, the ancient native race of fire-worshiping Zoroastrians.

In spite of additions and improvements to the Mission House (following an earthquake in 1830), the site's inadequacies were apparent. As the city expanded northward, the area became a poor working-class district, one of the least healthy in Tehran. By 1860 Charles Alison, the British minister, pressed for a new building in a new venue. By the summer of 1868, a new site of over 15 acres was found on what was popularly known as the Boulevard des Ambassadeurs (and more recently Ferdousi Avenue) as other foreign Missions followed the British example and acquired land. In the 1860s, it was still empty desert outside the city walls, and could be serviced by *qanats* bringing fresh water from the mountains.

The man in charge of the new complex was a British officer in the Bengal Engineers seconded to the staff of the Indo-European Telegraph Department, William Henry Pierson. He found his architect in London, James William Wild, who through a sojourn in Egypt and Damascus was already familiar with traditional Islamic architecture. The Legation was to be in a self-contained compound, facing inward behind high walls. The building ultimately constructed was in essence Italianate, asymmetrical, and a complicated composition of stepped-back levels, absorbing various Islamic elements, such as Persian windtowers and a wide-eaved *talar*. Pierson had the job of implementing the plans with a Persian workforce, which he achieved in spite of famine, cholera, and other difficulties. The Legation was finally ready in 1872.

Gertrude Bell visited her aunt there in 1892. She describes her arrival from the desert as if she had reached the Garden of Eden:

It was a very comfortable house built in the middle of it ... you can't think how lovely it all was outside, trees and trees and trees beneath them a froth of pink monthly roses (*Rosa chinensis* 'Old Blush'), climbing masses of briars, yellow or white or scarlet. Beds of dark red cabbage roses and hedges of great golden blooms. In the middle three deep tanks with weeping willows hanging over them from which runs a network of tiny water channels which the ten Zoroastrians who are the gardeners open and shut most cunningly, sluicing the flower beds with water.

Some of the plane trees planted by Pierson during the great famine of 1871–2 still survive, as described by Sacheverell Sitwell in 1956:

And what are strangely and perfectly beautiful are the trees. They are immensely tall—taller than any limes or elms ... and the same age as the houses. They are a kind of tree one has not seen before. Persian plane trees with silver stems, now leafless because it is the last week in March, make a lovely silvery pallor of tracery in the cold cloudless sky. One will never forget the silver plane trees which will always remind one of Tehran.

◆ *The British Embassy garden in Tehran, photograph ed in April 1970. Every spring the ambassador holds a "Wisteria Party" to celebrate the flowering of the vast plant which cascades over the lower verandah. Gertrude Bell found the garden enchanting when she visited in 1892.*

The plane trees of Tehran are the Asian plane, *Platanus orientalis*, from the Caspian forest. Although the London plane, *P.* × *hispanica* (a hybrid between *P. orientalis* and the American plane, *P. occidentalis*), with rapidly peeling bark, survives pollution best, the native plane requires less water.

By the 1900s Gulhak, the summer property in the mountains, had expanded to 45 acres with cool offices and verandahed houses to make the hot weather bearable. In the 1960s Iona Wright in *Black Sea Bride* described the garden as having a lawn, flowerbeds, and a blue-tiled pool, with potted oleanders on the verandah steps, lavenders and zinnias in the beds below. Again there were large Asian plane trees giving shade around the old-style Persian house. Nightingales sang in May and, later in the summer, golden orioles could be seen in the pine trees.

COURTYARD GARDENS

Wealthy merchants had long been making inner courtyard town gardens, in a domestic context, which offered shade and privacy to the family. By the 19th century, they joined the ranks of rulers and nobles in making grand pleasure gardens—venues for receptions and entertainment. In Persia private town dwellings, all with features typical of Islamic-Iranian domestic architecture, have always presented a modest façade to the narrow street far from the bazaar area. Although often with an imposing front door, they had no windows in the outer walls, and in the vestibule separate

passageways and stairs leading to the private *haram* and the public *biruni* were almost concealed. The *biruni* was the most elaborate room in the house, usually on the second floor, but sometimes a vaulted hall. The emphasis was on domestic privacy and the segregation of women. Each house formed a square with no access to its neighbors. An inner courtyard provided protection from wind, dust, and the worst of the sun's rays and was for family enjoyment. The walls were often decorated with delicate plasterwork, and the courtyard usually had a central pool surrounded by lush planting of trees and flowerbeds.

Today, some of these merchant houses, abandoned by the original families, with handsome *badgirs*, interior plasterwork, windows of colored glass (usually of Russian origin), mirrored walls, and courtyard gardens, have been restored. The Borujerdi House and the Tabataba'i House, hidden behind high walls in the southern part of the ancient city of Kashan, were built by 19th-century merchants. Typical of houses in desert towns, all the architectural detail is inside and the massive wooden entrance doors, each bearing two door knockers—a heavy one for the use of male visitors and a lighter one for females—are all that is visible from the street. As in most aristocratic town mansions, each house is designed as two distinct areas, the *andaruni* (the inner domestic quarter) and the *biruni* (the outer quarter for entertaining), each with a separate courtyard and pool and surrounding flowerbeds. The main reception hall of the *biruni*, on the first floor and two stories high, had ceilings of stucco carving and mirror work and windows with decorative colored glass that looked out onto a courtyard garden. In the basement was a *houz-khaneh* (pool house) for visiting in summer, containing water and fountains.

In Tabriz there are courtyard gardens at Behnam's House, built toward the end of the reign of Karim Khan Zand in the 18th century, and several others of the Qajar period, including a house built in 1868 which, because it was used for meetings in the course of the Constitutional Revolution in 1907–9, was later named Constitution House.

◆ *A glimpse of the main Tabataba'i courtyard garden,* ABOVE, *through the windows of the* talar, *the main reception hall of the* biruni. *Like the pierced screens found in Mughal buildings in India, patterned colored glass filters harsh sunlight and provides privacy.*
◆ *An inner courtyard of a 19th-century house in Tabriz,* LEFT, *overlooked by the arched windows of the reception hall.* ◆ *Separate door knockers are provided for male and female visitors,* OPPOSITE.

Tabataba'i House

The Tabataba'i mansion was built in 1834 for a carpet merchant, Seyed Jafar Tabataba'i. It was divided into two parts: the *andaruni*, with two inner courtyards and central pools, and the *biruni* where male guests were entertained. The rooms are decorated with elaborate plasterwork and colored glass typical of the Qajar period. Inner courtyards were reserved for family life and the private entrances were almost concealed in narrow dark passageways, making "surprise" openings into sunlit spaces containing water and flowers.

◆ *Interlacing plant forms and stylized cypresses,* ABOVE, *decorate the walls and columns in the main courtyard.* ◆ *The arched* talar, OPPOSITE BELOW, *framed by arcades and echoing the form of an* ayvan, *overlooks the garden's central rectangular pool and geometric flowerbeds.* ◆ *Pools in the courtyard of the* anderuni, OPPOSITE ABOVE LEFT, *reserved for outdoor living.* ◆ *Openings promote air circulation,* OPPOSITE ABOVE RIGHT, *and steps lead to the basement quarters which were used in summer.*

Borujerdi House

Built in 1855 by Haji Sayyed Hasan Natanzi, a merchant of Kashan, the Borujerdi House (or Khaneh-ye Borujerdiha) is distinguished by a six-sided *badgir*, pierced with openings which create a draft in the rooms below, and a large hall decorated with mirrors. The buildings are embellished throughout with plaster moldings of great delicacy that portray flowers and birds. A central courtyard, approached from a side entrance, has a pool, flanked by trees and flowerbeds, making a refuge to be enjoyed by the family.

◆ *The central courtyard,* RIGHT, *viewed from the reception hall, reflects the traditional* chahar bagh *pattern, with a pool flanked by grass panels planted with flowers and trees, including a Chinese bead tree* (Melia azedarach) *on the right. A four-sided* badgir *tunnels breezes to the rooms beneath.* ◆ ABOVE *The domed ceiling of the two-story reception hall.*

8 The Persian legacy

"*They set stone flowers in the marble*
That by their colour, if not their perfume,
surpass real flowers." Abu Talib Kalim

 FROM THE MID-7TH CENTURY ONWARD THE CORE OF THE ISLAMIC WORLD WAS IN SYRIA, Egypt, and the Mesopotamian area, including Iraq, and the Persian Empire, mainly desert countries where the concept of the early oasis garden readily adapted to the spiritual ideal revealed by the Koran. Inspired by a love of flowers and the great Sasanian gardens they had discovered as they spread west from Mecca and Medina, the Muslims carried a garden tradition with them as their empire expanded, a tradition which could be adapted in different climatic and topographical regions. Within a hundred years of their early conquests, the Arabs had taken the new Islamic faith through the Levant in the west to North Africa and into southern Spain, as well as to Central Asia in the east. By the 16th century, Babur and his descendants consolidated the Mughal Empire in northern India, and by the 17th century the Ottoman sultans had carried the Muslim faith through the Balkans to the gates of Vienna.

Whereas in desert lands the watered oasis was a refuge from thirst and death, in the fertile lands of the Iberian peninsula gardens reflected surrounding agriculture. On the dusty plains of Hindustan, royal gardens were symbols of divinely sanctioned rule, and, as grand settings for tombs, symbols of the afterlife. In the valleys of Kashmir, abundant water allowed gardens unprecedented beauty. Over future centuries, even without Koranic significance, the enclosed garden, originating in ancient Persia, became a model for garden-makers in the West, a place where ordered reality offered relief from the stresses of everyday life.

MOORISH GARDENS

The geometric gardens of the Moors (as the Muslims became known in Spain)—basically four-fold designs of paths and channels, with pools, sunken flowerbeds, terraces, and pavilions with shady porticoes—were to include the most exquisite gardens yet seen in Europe. In the rich farming lands of southern Spain, they reflected the pattern of productive fields around them, celebrating earthly success rather than contrasting with hostile desert. Initially, however, when the Berbers, Muslims from North Africa, swept through al-Andalus in 711, they found an almost barren landscape. Since the decline of the Roman Empire, the area had suffered from centuries of wars, divided government, famine, and plague. For several decades the Muslim state in Spain was ruled by caliphs from Damascus, but from 755 it began to flourish under independent Umayyad rulers, the first of whom, prince 'Abd al-Rahman I, had escaped assassination during the 'Abbasid coup of 750. Ancient aqueducts were mended and the Umayyads reintroduced sophisticated irrigation systems derived from Rome and Persia. They fertilized the land and encouraged investment in trees and orchards, restoring prosperity to the countryside.

Ideas from Greek and Roman civilizations fused with an architectural style derived from the Iranian lands of Persia and Central Asia to create gardens for sumptuous living, planted with exotic fruits and flowers, many brought from the eastern end of the Mediterranean and from as far east as Persia, India, and China. As well as being sacred representations of Paradise and pleasure parks for royalty, they expressed an ideal happiness for man. Some were courtyards inspired by the Persian *chahar bagh*, divided into four by decorative rather than functional water rills. In southern regions the Berbers planted groves of fruiting palms around natural pools—derived from their *aghal* (North African oasis garden)—but they were designed for beauty and repose, often appearing as sophisticated extensions of the cultivated landscape. Open fields and gardens built around dwelling houses or palaces were integrated, more akin to the Renaissance gardens of Italy where the concept of a "villa" included a dwelling house, the garden, storage for grain, wine, and fruits, and the productive fields, all intimately connected. Outside the towns, walled orchard gardens, known as *bostan* in Persia and *hadiqa* in Arabic, divided by water channels, were a form of productive agriculture on a small scale, very similar to the Latin *hortus*.

The Umayyad Caliph 'Abd al-Rahman I began building

◆ PRECEDING PAGES *The garden to the south of the Taj Mahal is laid-out like a Persian* chahar bagh *with water channels dividing the space into quadrants.* ◆ *Ranks of orange trees in the Patio de los Naranjos,* ABOVE, *continue the rhythm of the columns inside the Grand Mosque at Cordoba, built in the 780s and now a Christian cathedral.*

Cordoba's magnificent Grand Mosque in the 780s, its arcades opening onto the Patio de los Naranjos (Courtyard of Oranges), which is the earliest surviving Hispano-Islamic garden and possibly the oldest extant garden in Europe. Orange trees in well-ordered ranks, reflecting the forest-like rhythm of the mosque's red and white columns, recall Cyrus the Younger's 5th-century BC park at Sardis. A grid system of irrigation canals set in the brick floor adds further regimentation.

Arruzafa near Cordoba, where 'Abd al-Rahman I conducted experiments in fruit and flower growing, may have been modeled on his grandfather's palatial complex at Rusafa near Raqqa in Syria, which dated to 724–43. With a raised pavilion set in a four-fold garden, Rusafa is the earliest example of a cross-axial garden in the Islamic world. In a plaintive poem, ar-Rahman expressed yearning for his native Syria, sympathizing with "the lonely palm tree in the midst of Arruzafa, here in the west, far from its land … let the morning rain from the scurrying clouds fall upon you, their waters spilling upon you, and let the stars weep their tears upon you."

The Muslim colony rapidly spread through an area much greater than modern Andalusia, the boundaries, after excursions into France, ultimately settling around an area that included Toledo, Seville, and Granada, where water from melting snows in the sierra fed the great rivers flowing through the valleys and plains. By the 10th century the capital city of Cordoba had become the center of scholarship in western Europe, a rival to 'Abbasid Baghdad at a time when the rest of Europe was in cultural decline. The city attracted classicists, philosophers, poets, doctors, and botanists. Its poets expressed a sensitive attitude to nature's unadorned beauty (whereas contemporary poets in Persia confined their nature imagery to the artificially created garden.) Arab scholarship, showing considerable botanical expertise, was gradually absorbed across the Pyrenees, with bulbs, seeds, cuttings, and roots of plants carried by returning pilgrims to northern Europe. However, although Persian-style parks

in Sicily inspired Robert of Artois's 13th-century park at Hesdin in northern France, the water-based Islamic garden did not, in general, become a model for the few gardens developing in medieval Europe.

Abbasid influences, with information brought by travelers, remained strong in southern Spain during the 10th century. In particular, the 9th-century palaces of Samarra on the Tigris appear to have been the prototype for vast Ummayyad palace complexes with interconnecting courtyards where huge square tanks of reflecting water doubled dimensions by optical illusion. In 936 'Abd al-Rahman III began his palatial garden city of Madinat az-Zahra, set in a green and watered landscape outside Cordoba. He spent forty years laying out a vast network of palaces, reception halls, gardens, administrative offices, and stables, its grand concept reminiscent of the pre-Islamic Sasanian imperial gardens in Persia. Pools were fed with water from the sierra, brought by aqueducts similar to those excavated at Samarra. Certain features, such as the mercury pool, seem to have been drawn from the late-9th-century Tulunid palace at Al-Qatai in Egypt, which included a magnificent garden that, with watercourses running through opulent courtyards, bore a distinct resemblance to palaces at Samarra.

Built on descending terraces, Madinat az-Zahra's royal pavilions, throne rooms, and towers formed a series of *basatin that manazirihi* (Arabic, meaning "a place from which to gaze") or mirador (Spanish, meaning literally "a place for looking.") These elements combined to give a vision of the whole garden city, a concept inaugurated by Baghdad's first caliph with his viewpoints and belvederes. Viewpoints also directed the eye beyond the walls to the surrounding valley, thus setting a precedent for the Nasrid fortress of the Alhambra at Granada, where towers and miradors incorporated vistas of the Generalife garden across the valley and stupendous views of the snow-covered peaks of the Sierra Nevada. The Salon Rico (reception hall) at Madinat az-Zahra opened to the south, with five horseshoe arches on columns directing the eye into the quadripartite garden and across the pool to the pavilion, which appeared to be floating on water. The interlinked palaces and gardens at Madinat az-Zahra, the association between water and architecture, and the garden city's political significance as a center of power, had immense influence on contemporary and future developments (and in particular on the Mughul emperors in India in the 16th century). Buildings reflected in still water tanks appeared to be doubled, like the columns at the Chehel Sotun in Isfahan and the Taj Mahal at Agra.

Arruzafa and Madinat az-Zahra were destroyed when Berbers captured Cordoba in 1010. Toledo became the hub of horticultural activity. Excavation at the Huerta del Rey (King's Garden) in Toledo, conceived by Ibn Wafid (999–1008) and maintained by his successor Ibn Bassal until 1085, has revealed that the garden had a wheel that raised water from the River Tagus to make a pool. A cascade fell like a curtain over the crystal pavilion in the center of the pool.

Both Ibn Wafid and Ibn Bassal studied plants as well as methods of gardening. A hundred years later, Abu Zakarriyya Yahya Ibn al 'Awwam drew on their work in his *Kitab al-filaha* (Book of Agriculture), which broke new ground in suggesting some garden design principles, including cypresses to mark corners and as avenues along main walks, cedars and pines to make shady alleys, and hedges of box and bay laurel. In a poem describing the layout of pleasure gardens composed in 1348, Ibn Loyun developed the ideas in al 'Awwam's *Kitab al-filaha*. He advocates setting the house in an elevated position, with a southern aspect: "Choose the dominant position to build a house and garden to better keep watch and defend it," he writes, and "it should face the midday sun." He suggests the door be "placed laterally," confirming the Moors' preference for a modest side entrance rather than the Persian monumental doorway aligned with garden pools. He continues:

• In the 13th-century Spanish story of Bayard and Riyad, ABOVE, Bayard lies unconscious beside a noria, a hinged wheel used for raising rapidly moving water without animal power. • In the Patio de los Arrayanes (Court of Myrtles), OPPOSITE, at the Alhambra, the Hall of the Ambassadors is reflected in the pool. The decorations on the marble-columned arcades include Koranic inscriptions.

The well or pool should be slightly raised, and there should be a canal running under the shade of trees … near at hand, beds will be planted with evergreens of all varieties that will brighten the view, and further on flowers of many kinds and evergreen trees … it will be longer than it is broad so that the eye will not tire in its contemplation … a pavilion will be set aside in the lower part for guests who come to bear company to its master.

As the Umayyads lost power and the kingdom was weakened by feuds between minor kings, Toledo fell into Christian hands in 1085 and Seville in 1248, leaving Granada isolated as a small sultanate, ruled by the Nasrids who came to power in 1232, their territories including Granada and extending to Almeria and Malaga on the coast. Until conquered in 1492, Granada was the final stronghold of the Arabs in Spain, its citadel, palaces, and gardens offering the last echo of Moorish splendor in a kingdom hemmed in by hostile Christendom. The great Hispano-Islamic gardens at the Generalife and Alhambra, built by the Nasrids in the 13th and 14th centuries, represented the ultimate refuge as the area of Muslim-ruled Andalusia decreased, their compartments, like unroofed enclosures, inward-looking except for the miradors allowing outward views. They owed considerable debts to the Madinat az-Zahra and, although heavily restored during the last two centuries, retain their beauty. Set high in the hills, where they receive breezes from snow-covered mountains, the inner gardens are, nevertheless, concealed behind walls and elegant façades. Still water reflecting the richly carved stuccoed arches and marble columns feeds narrow marble channels and, rushing beneath shaded colonnades, bubbles in basins to bring movement to the peaceful atmosphere. The great 14th-century traveler Ibn Battuta visited Granada in the late 1340s and paid tribute to the abundance of beautiful estates with gardens and pavilions. Plant lists, including fruits and exotic as well as native flowers, compiled by Spanish botanists in

the 11th and 12th centuries, and treatises on husbandry help us to visualize the planted gardens.

In 1492 Granada fell to Catholic forces under Ferdinand and Isabella and the Moors were finally driven from Spain. Most of the refugees escaped to North Africa, giving impetus there to the building of Hispano-Islamic-type mosques, palaces, and gardens along the coast, territory that was to become part of the Ottoman Empire in the 16th century. The legacy is still evident in southern Spain, both in the buildings and garden architecture; today, water bubbles in the center of the flower-filled courtyards of Cordoba. Its influence spread to the New World, to enclosed mission and 20th-century gardens in California and Arizona which reflect the "desert" ethos.

Generalife

The Generalife was a summer pleasance built by the Nasrid Muhammad III during the first years of the 14th century, on the side of the Santa Elena hill in view of the Alhambra. Early descriptions of its layout and planting were written by the Venetian traveler Andres Navagero, who visited both the Generalife and the Alhambra between 1524 and 1526, within fifty years of the 1492 Christian conquest.

Unlike the Alhambra with its enclosed "rooms," the Generalife is draped over the terraced hillside and open to fresh mountain winds. Its only secluded courtyard, the Acequia Court, or Canal Court, is on a horizontal plane at the base of the slope. Water was carried diagonally across the higher orchards, and down the scalloped channels of balustrading of a steep stairway, past the secluded Garden of the Sultana, to feed the central canal (the arching water spouts are a 19th-century addition). This water was supplemented by a waterwheel in a tower in the Huerta de la Merceria. After a fire in the 1950s, the Acequia Court was excavated and the original layout and levels were revealed. Based on the Persian quadripartite system, the longer axis stretched northwest to the North Pavilion and a much shorter east-west axis crossed the center. The flower-beds were set about 2 feet 5 inches below the existing pavements. Archaeologists discovered that the garden must originally have been planted with low-growing flowers requiring little soil, although there were some deeper pits obviously made for shrubs, such as myrtle, and orange trees which had been described as growing there in the 16th century. After the excavations the soil was returned to the Acequia Court, and today modern annuals with no historical authenticity give a colorful display.

Along the west side a projecting mirador framed a magnificent view of the Alhambra complex to the west. To the south was the three-storied harem.

♦ *The Patio de la Acequia in the gardens of the Generalife was originally laid out in a traditional* chahar bagh *pattern, divided into quadrants by water rills, with sunken beds for flowers and fruit trees. Today, the garden has a single central water channel with flanking flowerbeds at the same level, planted with modern flowers. Set below a hillside, the court's water is brought to the north pavilion diagonally across the slope and down a water stairway with open scalloped channels. The arching water jets are a 19th-century innovation.*

The 16th- and 17th-century Mughal gardens of northern India and Kashmir, which derived their Persian-style architecture directly from Iranian lands, represent the pinnacle of Muslim grandeur. Just as the Islamic conquerors had absorbed Persian culture in the 7th and 8th centuries, the Mughal Emperors adopted Persian ways, with Persian as the official language and craftsmen from Persia influencing the development of painting, poetry, and architecture.

Imbued with a love and appreciation of nature, the Mughals filled their gardens with flowers—spring-flowering bulbs from Kabul and Kashmir grew under the low canopies of orchard fruit among fields of clover. Trees, such as tall evergreen neem (*Azadirachta indica*), tamarind (*Tamarindus indica*), banyan (*Ficus benghalensisi*), and another fig, the pipal (*Ficus religiosa*), Buddha's sacred tree under which he obtained perfect knowledge, marked the corners to provide deep shade. Today, although little attempt is made to grow the authentic trees and flowers of the Mughal period, water seldom flows in the wide water channels, and no fountains sparkle in the sun, enough remains to conjure the days of glory.

Babur, the founder of the Mughal Empire, was born in Ferghana in Transoxiana. As a boy he had visited the Timurid capital at Samarkand and seen gardens that were to shape his destiny—both as a conqueror and as a lover of the natural world. His early life was spent in an ultimately unsuccessful struggle to recover Samarkand and regain his inheritance as a descendant of Timur. Babur's first gardens—variants on the enclosed *chahar bagh*, and on the orchard gardens of the Timurids—were made on the hillsides around Kabul, the city he captured in 1504. In his memoirs of struggles and conquests, the *Babur-nameh*, he describes the Bagh-e Vafa (Garden of Fidelity) set in a valley near the old city of Jalalabad

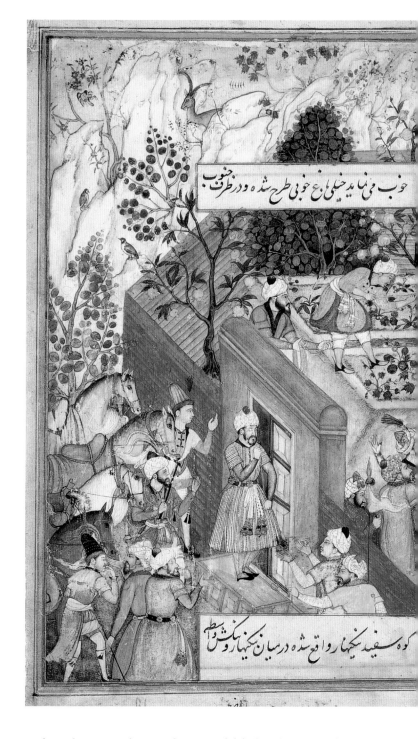

◆ *The Bagh-e Vafa, Babur's garden near Jalalabad made in the early 16th century, had a traditional Persian* chahar bagh *layout, with water-courses dividing the walled garden into quadrants and emptying into a basin. The miniature, dated 1680, shows Babur directing his gardeners and his garden architect, who holds a plan of the garden, while envoys at the entrance portal await an audience.*

was so beautiful that "it was such that no painter trying to depict it could have equalled it." He planted pomegranates, oranges, and citrons in the garden and later added plantains (bananas), other fruit trees, and sugar cane.

The *Babur-nameh* includes many references to garden making, flowers, and trees, often mentioning wildflowers such as tulips growing in the mountains. He believed no garden should be without water and, when necessary, would straighten a natural streambed to make it conform to the traditional garden pattern.

After the failure of his final attempt on Samarkand in 1512, Babur began raids southward, establishing the Mughal Empire in 1526 with the overthrow of the Sultan of Delhi. Compared with Kabul's more temperate, mountain climate, the plains of Hindustan were hot and dusty, "so bad and unattractive," Babur wrote, that "we traversed them with a hundred disgusts and repulsions." The gardens he found were irrigated by the Indus, Jumna, and Ganges Rivers, the water raised with oxen-driven wheels, introduced by a Persian engineer in the 11th century, and conserved in storage tanks for use in the dry season. In a different climate and, without the need for the artificial irrigation canals that dictated the pattern of desert gardens, they lacked the geometrically planned symmetry of the enclosed Persian *pairidaeza* and Timurid orchards. Babur at once started to make gardens for his peripatetic court, introducing the ordered esthetic of the Persian garden into the Indian context. By appropriating lands outside the fortresses of the pre-Mughal rulers whom he had defeated, he demonstrated to the Hindu majority his unassailable territorial power. As settings for dazzling receptions, in which a strict code allowed both public and private access to the royal presence, the imperial gardens he

(the ancient Nysa of Alexander). For three or four days in late summer, Babur camped in the four-fold garden, where intersecting watercourses opened out into a square pool: "Those were the days of the garden's beauty," he writes "its lawns were one sheet of trefoil; its pomegranate trees yellowed to autumn splendour." By November an apple tree

established—camp-like enclosures in Timurid style—became more potent as symbols of royal power and prestige than as representations of the Koranic Paradise.

Babur encouraged his nobles to lay out gardens along the Jumna River in Agra, creating a suburb of gardens much like those at Samarkand and Herat. In both Agra and Delhi, waterfront gardens became a feature, with their main buildings set on the riverbank, where they could receive cooling breezes and be seen by passing boats, rather than in the center or cross-axis of the garden. The gardens, in traditional form with water channels parallel and at right angles, stretched out behind, the water raised from the Jumna with rotating wheels powered by oxen. One of the gardens remaining on the east side of the river at Agra, the Hasht Behesht (Eight Paradises) is attributed to Babur himself, but his part in its making is uncorroborated. However, the site of the massive terraced Bagh-e Nilufar (Lotus Pool Garden) at Dholpur south of Agra, built between 1526 and his death in 1530, was identified in 1978 from the description in the *Babur-nameh*. A lotus-shaped pool, cut from an outcrop of red sandstone, a small *chadar*, and the remains of an aqueduct can still be seen.

From imperial archives we know that Babur's sons, grandsons, and great-grandsons built gardens all over the empire. On campaigns—a lot of time was spent controlling uprisings—they met and rested in gardens with their court and tented armies. While maintaining the canonical layout, gardens acquired a variety of functional elements, fulfilling the evermore-elaborate rules of court etiquette, to become increasingly magnificent symbols of the dynasty. Walls were inlaid with floral patterns of jewels and semi-precious stones and marble reliefs of flowers decorated entrance halls and tombs.

Babur's son, Homayun, spent many years of his reign in exile with Shah Tahmasp in Persia, returning to Delhi for only a year before his death there from a fall in his library in 1556. His successor, Akbar (1542–1606), consolidated the Mughal Empire and is remembered for his religious toler-

ance and his buildings reflecting Hindu influence, while his gardens, although retaining their symmetrical geometry, evolved with wider channels of water and paved walkways. The first major project of his reign was the construction, with his father's widow, a Persian, of Homayun's tomb in Delhi. With a central Persian-style *ayvan*, the mausoleum emphasized the power of the Mughal invaders and their dynastic inheritance. It was surrounded by an equally Persian-style *chahar bagh* garden—a vast area of sandstone-paved walkways, narrow channels of water, and open tanks—which reconfirmed the Paradise metaphor associated with the afterlife. Akbar began constructing his own tomb at Sikandra, which was completed by his son Jahangir (1569–1627). The sandstone mausoleum is inlaid with decorative white marble and set in the center of a vast four-fold garden, its purpose clear from the inscription over the gate: "These are the Gardens of Paradise; enter them to dwell therein eternally."

For his complex of palaces and gardens at Fathepur Sikri, south of Agra, Akbar imported quantities of trees and flowers for the sunken flowerbeds beside the watercourses that burbled between sandstone pavements. Under his grandson Shah Jahan (1592–1666), the palace gardens at the Red Fort in Agra, with wide water channels and paved walkways inspired by the Madinat az-Zahra in Cordoba, became increasingly magnificent symbols of the Mughal dynasty. The monolithic entrance gateway led into a vast courtyard terminating in the Divan-e 'Amm (Audience Hall), decorated with sumptuous silk and velvet hangings, the floors covered with rich carpets and cushions. Here the public could see the emperor on his throne after the first prayers of the day. A second sighting took place in the Divan-e Khas (Private Pavilion), where he received members of his court and administrative matters were discussed.

After Akbar's conquest of Kashmir in 1586, the Mughals built terraced gardens on a vast scale in idyllic valleys, below mountain slopes clad with deodars, around Shrinagar and Lake Dal. Here, far from the dusty Indian plains, he and

Homayun's tomb and surrounding gardens, near the Jumna River in Delhi, were constructed by his widow and his successor, Emperor Akbar, between 1562 and 1571. The monumental building was designed by the son of Mirak Sayyid Ghiyas, a builder in late-Timurid Herat who had joined Babur in India in 1529. The Persian-style chahar bagh *was laid out with water channels flanked by red sandstone and sunken beds for fruit trees and flowers. Today Homayun's tomb garden is under restoration by the Aga Khan Foundation.*

subsequent emperors liked to spend the hot season. With a limitless supply of water, perfect summer weather, and more than adequate riches, they installed canals and walk-ways on different levels, connected by rippling *chadars* behind which candles or lamps were concealed in niches to make the shimmering curtains of water glow at night. Pavilions, built above cascades, appeared to float on the water. Akbar crossed the tortuous mountain passes to the valley of Kashmir three times during his reign. At 2,500 feet above sea level, the air was crisp and he loved Lake Dal, with its floating islands of vegetation, and to watch the saffron being harvested in the fall. He planted a thousand plane trees in the Nasim Bagh on the lakeshore at Shrinagar and started building a palace, which was used by later emperors as a summer residence.

The pleasure-loving Jahangir, a wine and opium addict, was a great garden and nature lover. For E'timad ad-Douuleh, the father of his Persian queen Nur Jahan, he built between 1622 and 1628 one of the most distinguished tomb gardens in Agra. It was a *chahar bagh* with water channels and flower-beds, in the center of which stood a white marble mausoleum decorated with inlays of semi-precious stones and marble bas-reliefs of flowers. With his wife, Jahangir also spent much time extending the gardens of Shalimar, Achabal, and Verinag in Kashmir, recording his delight in colorful descriptions:

> Kashmir is a garden of eternal spring ... a delightful flower-bed ... Its pleasant meads and enchanting cascades are beyond all description. There are running streams and fountains beyond count. Where ever the eye reaches, there are verdure and running water.

Jahangir employed Mansur to portray the wild flowers of Kashmir in a hundred paintings.

The royal gardens in Kashmir begun by Jahangir were completed by Shah Jahan (1628–57). By the middle of the 17th century there were reputed to be 777 gardens, including Nur Jahan's own Bagh-e Jarogha and, the most spectacular of all, Bagh-e Neshat, developed by her brother Asaf Khan. In *Travels in the Moghul Empire*,

François Bernier, who visited Kashmir in March 1665 with Jahangir's grandson Auranzib, describes the whole kingdom as "a fertile and highly cultivated garden ... meadows and vineyards, fields of rice, wheat, hemp, saffron and many sorts of vegetables ... intermingled with trenches filled with

◆ *The Shalimar Bagh on Lake Dal, built by Jahangir in 1619, extended the traditional* chahar bagh *formula and, exploiting the abundant supply of water in Kashmir, included torrential cascades and* chadars. *The garden, approached from the lake, contained audience halls, the Divan-e 'Amm and the Divan-e Khas, and a black marble pavilion surrounded by water and roofed, in Kashmir style, in wood, which served as the women's quarters.*

water, rivulets, canals and several small lakes, vary the enchanting scene." He considered Shalimar Bagh to be the most beautiful of all the gardens. Approached by *shikara* (boat),

> the entrance from the lake is through a spacious canal, bordered with green turf, and running between two rows of poplars…it leads to a large summer-house placed in the middle of the garden. A second canal still finer than the first, then conducts you to another summer-house, at the end of the garden. In the middle [of the canal] is a long row of fountains, fifteen paces asunder; besides which there are … large circular basins … out of which arise other fountains, formed into a variety of shapes and figures.

By the beginning of the 1630s, Shah Jahan had assembled designers and craftsmen from all over India, Persia, and Central Asia to construct the Taj Mahal which was to be the masterpiece of the Mughal dynasty and the ultimate expression of architectural perfection. The tomb for his favorite wife, Mumtaz Mahal, was built of shimmering white marble and framed by slender minarets, its walls inlaid with semi-precious stones. Set on a terrace above the Jumna River at the end of a long *chahar bagh*, and doubled in size by its reflection in the central water channel, the mausoleum appeared to float between the paradise garden and the river landscape below. With canals representing the four rivers of Paradise, cypress avenues symbolizing immortality, and fruit trees and flower-filled parterres evoking regeneration, it was the perfect metaphor of the afterlife. Unfortunately, Lord Curzon's restoration involved filling in the sunken beds.

By the middle of the 17th century, as Shah Jahan's reign came to a close, Mughal culture reached its peak. During the reign of his son Auranzib, from 1658 to 1707, a stricter adherence to the Muslim faith meant a return to the more sacred, less luxurious interpretation of garden making. After his death the dynasty gradually faded to oblivion under British administration.

THE TASTE
FOR EASTERN CULTURE

165

♦
♦

THE
PERSIAN
LEGACY

The preoccupation of Western civilization with the Islamic world and Eastern culture has existed since contacts, sometimes hostile but often purely commercial, were first made. Just as the Roman generals brought back tales of the opulent palaces and splendid hunting parks of pre-Islamic Persia, the Crusaders acquired beautiful and luxurious objects, manufactured in Baghdad since the 'Abbasid period but unknown in the West, to satisfy the growing wealth of both the feudal nobility and the urban bourgeoisie in Europe. After 1453 political *rapprochement* with the Ottoman empire made trade with the East easier, with Europe benefiting from imports of exotic materials: silks, brocades, lacquers, carpets, ceramics, glass, and, by 1600, bulbous plants from the Anatolian and Persian mountains. The colorful hangings, cushions, and rugs which originally decorated nomad tents were woven in more delicate materials. In medieval Venice architectural styles had a marked Islamic flavor, especially in the 13th- to 15th-century work on the façade of St Mark's and the Doge's Palace, an obvious link achieved by the extensive trading privileges which the Serene Republic had acquired throughout the Mediterranean, although by 1300 trade with Mongol-ruled Persia was more limited.

It was not until the 17th century, however, that the romantic lure of Islamic architecture, sculpture, and painting began to attract Europeans in general, by then able to travel within the Ottoman and Persian lands and beyond to the Mughal Empire in India. Travelers and merchants brought back tales of mosques, palaces, untold riches, and fabulous jewels, as well as images of the seductive Muslim gardens of Isfahan and the Mughal court. But, strangely, the new enthusiasm for the exotic in gardens and their inter-relationship with buildings did not lead to a European interest in reproducing the enclosed Persian gardens. Possibly it was felt that the Persian garden needed a desert setting, keeping harsh nature at bay, while in Europe,

Renaissance humanist thought had already stimulated a more intimate relationship between man and the natural world, with gardens linked to the outer landscape.

Islamic-style pavilions and Turkish mosques and tents, as well as Chinese tea houses, were introduced into Europe's new 18th-century landscape parks. Placed as focal points to be revealed in a circuit walk with no spatial relationship to their settings, they were surprise incidents in an allegorical interpretation. Charles Hamilton's Turkish tent at Painshill and the even grander example at Haga Park in Sweden, designed by Frederick Magnus Piper for Gustavus III, were isolated elements. A whole Turkish mosque at Schwetzingen in Germany, designed by Nicolas de Pigage in 1795, had its own garden around it with no hint of the East, being merely a part of the grand re-ordering of the original baroque park into an ideal rococo landscape. Another Turkish mosque in the gardens of Potsdam was created in the 1840s and a Moorish garden inspired by the Alhambra was designed for William I in 1842 in the Wilhelma Park at Stuttgart. Monumental in design, it included many features reminiscent of 14th-century Andalusia but lacked the intimate and almost spiritual ambience of the enclosed Spanish gardens.

While Europeans considered Islamic art as no more than exotic decoration, by the early 19th century India, its Mughal art and architecture, had admirers in Britain among homecoming Indian nabobs. Having made their fortune privately or through working for the East India Company, they sought to recapture an Indian ambience by introducing Mughal architecture into the English countryside. Both Sezincote and Dalesford in Gloucestershire were built as Indian-type palaces

incorporating Mughal architectural features. Sezincote was designed in about 1805 by the architect Samuel Pepys Cockerell for his brother Sir Charles Cockerell who had resided for many years in Bengal, and Humphry Repton gave advice on the garden, although his plans were not used. William Hodge's aquatints of Indian scenery, published in 1788, and *Oriental Scenery*, a series of prints by Thomas and William Daniell showing Hindu and Mughal architecture, were sources for decorative detail both in buildings and garden work. With a golden onion dome, an octagon pavilion at the end of the conservatory, and an imposing *ayvan*-type entrance in the east elevation, as well as windows framed by Mughal arches, Sezincote remains the most imposing

♦ At Filoli, ABOVE, *near San Francisco in California, created in the 1920s, geometric compartments recall the gardens of Italy, but the ambience is Islamic, with a central reflecting pool, verdant lawns, trees and flowers set in the relatively dry countryside, evoking an oasis in the desert.* ♦ The Indian-style house at Sezincote in Gloucestershire, OPPOSITE, *designed in the early 19th century, was enriched by a Mughal garden created by Sir Cyril and Lady Kleinwort after 1944. Irish yews take the place of cypresses to flank a narrow rill and raised octagonal pool.*

example of country-house "Indian" architecture in England. Unfortunately, although there were Indian motifs in the garden, no attempt was made to introduce elements of the ordered Islamic garden, clearly considered to be distinctly alien in an English park. Sezincote had to wait to the last half of the 20th century for a new Indian-style garden to be designed by Sir Cyril and Lady Kleinwort, who had bought the house in 1944. On the lawn below the curving Orangery, staccato yews now line a narrow north-south water channel, with a raised octagonal pool in the center, in which the onion-shaped dome of the house is reflected.

The taste for romantic Eastern culture, with its erotic overtones, seems to have been considered a luxurious folly by Europeans deep into Renaissance philosophy. For a flower garden at Valleyfield in Fife, Scotland, Repton's design in *Observations on the Theory and Practice of Landscape Gardening* (1803) is a formal walled enclosure with a distinctly Persian look—a long water tank aligned on a pavilion and a trelliswork arbor—for which he feels bound to apologize: "in an open park anything obviously artificial is to be avoided, in an enclosed garden it harmonizes where

everything else is artificial." His 1806 design for the garden of the Royal Pavilion at Brighton for the Prince Regent included Indian features, such as a "Hindu"-style rectangular pool approached by steps between domed kiosks, but the commission went to John Nash. In the 1840s an "Alhambra Garden" was made at Elvaston Castle in Derbyshire. A chromolithograph of 1857 by E. Adveno Brooke shows that it was Muslim only by name.

It was not until the turn of the 20th century that English architects such as Edwin Lutyens and Harold Peto struck a new chord with gardens that, without a religious connotation, captured something of the spirit of the Persian and Islamic gardens, with simple axial water channels aligned on a pavilion. Peto's grand water garden at Buscot Park in Oxfordshire had a strong Mughal ambience, resembling gardens in Kashmir. At La Mortella on the island of Ischia near Naples in the 1970s Russell Page designed the lower garden with Islamic-type pools and water rills. Most other designers, such as Norah Lindsay, considered Persian gardens in terms of decorative garden carpets and used historic nuance to create exquisitely patterned flower gardens.

In the 21st century the enclosed Persian garden provides a model for gardeners in search of individual interpretations of paradise. The ordered pattern of its fourfold layout, with murmuring water to soothe the soul, trees for shade, and flowers for both color and scent, has parallels with the Mughal concept of control over a peaceful kingdom. Today's gardeners seeking to create secluded havens as antidotes to the bustle of modern life are following a tradition that began in Persia at least 2,500 years ago in the garden of Cyrus the Great at Pasargadae.

◆ *Fernando Caruncho's design for Camp Sarch in Minorca, ABOVE, constructed between 1989 and 2000, includes Moorish-style water parterres alternating with sculptural clipped evergreen escallonia and pistachio, each square separated by stone walkways.* ◆ *Helen Dillon has replaced a manicured lawn with an Islamic-style pool, constructed of white Irish limestone, in the center of her Dublin garden, OPPOSITE. Separated from the outside world, the town garden evokes the essence of the spiritual Paradise to come as revealed in the Koran, a place for contemplation and repose in which to anticipate the pleasures of the afterlife.*

Quatre Vents

The garden of Francis and Anne Cabot, created in the late 20th century near the St Lawrence River, north of Quebec, with reflecting canals, pools, and rills, enclosed by tall hedges and avenues of evergreens, evokes the spirit of Persian and Islamic gardens. Clipped thuja—the only evergreen which withstands the hard Canadian winters—takes the place of the fastigiate cypresses of gardens in Iran, demonstrating how a historical and cultural style can be transferred to a very different climate. Rather than being enclosed as a refuge from thirst and arid desert, Les Quatre Vents "borrows" the surrounding landscape which, as in the Moorish gardens of Spain and the Mughal gardens of Kashmir, is integral to the design.

As well as the wild landscape of the Laurentian hills beyond the garden's perimeter, the Cabots' garden is large enough to incorporate areas of wilderness within that alternate and contrast with the formality of enclosed "inner" compartments. Swaying bridges cross ravines, a Chinese moon-bridge is mirrored in a pond edged with native flowers, a sweeping meadow spreads out before a view over the St Lawrence River, informal woodland beds are filled with plants, many of which are of botanical interest, and at the base of the ravine there is a Japanese tea house.

✦ *The tall French-style* pigeonnier, ABOVE, *overlooks a narrow canal and frames views of wild countryside.* ✦ *Like a Spanish mirador, the arch,* OPPOSITE RIGHT, *directs the eye beyond the garden and, reflected in the canal, duplicates the central water feature to increase the feeling of dimension and distance.* ✦ *Nearest the house, a thuja walk,* OPPOSITE LEFT, *encloses rills and basins, opening and narrowing in sequence like the watercourses in Cyrus the Great's garden at Pasargadae, created in the 6th century BC.*

Notes for travelers in Iran

Most western tourists begin and end visits to Iran in Tehran where the study of both pre-Islamic and Islamic artifacts in the museums is essential before and after traveling in the country. The order of the notes that follow reflects the way tours from Tehran tend to be organized.

Tehran: Province of Tehran

Tehran has been the capital of Iran for only two centuries. Most traces of its earlier history have vanished, with modern boulevards driven through the medieval streets. The two most important Qajar palaces in the city, the Negarestan and Qasr-e Farahabad, their grand gardens laid out in a traditional Persian style, have been demolished (see Chapter 7).

GOLESTAN PALACE The main entrance to the palace, Dar-e Sa'adat (Gate of Happiness), gives a view of a rectangular pool, lined with plane trees, in front of the Divan Khaneh (Audience Hall), where the Takht-e Marmar (Marble Throne) is still displayed. (The so-called Peacock Throne is now housed, with the Iranian crown jewels, in the vaults of the Melli Bank.) The last Pahlavi Shah was crowned in the Divan Khaneh in 1967, by which time most of the inner complex had been converted into museum galleries and offices, including

Tehran: Golestan Palace

the Ethnographical Museum near the main entrance. The garden was divided by several buildings, which were pulled down in 1875 by Naser ad-Din Shah at the time he inaugurated part of an adjacent reception area as a museum, where today paintings of the Golestan Palace and other Qajar gardens are on display, with European objects picked up by the Shah on visits to Europe. His European-style twin-towered building, the Shams al-'Emareh, its façade originally reflected in a large basin (now vanished), still stands at the eastern side of the complex. Currently, the garden is not well maintained. Open to the public.

National Botanic Garden of Iran: the rock garden

The Northern Slopes: Province of Tehran

The summer resorts built by rulers and Persian nobles on the lower slopes of the Alborz to the north of the city during the 19th century are in an area now swallowed up by suburbs. Villa sites developed in mountain districts such as Tajrish and Niavaran are mostly in ruins, but steps, pillars, and stone channels hidden in the woods evoke past glories.

SAHEBQARANIEH PALACE Built after the middle of the 19th century by Naser ad-Din Shah, the palace at Niavaran offers a superb view over the city. Descending terraces show evidence of Persian style. Open to the public.

BAGH-E MALEK Situated on the steep slopes below the village of Golabdarreh, the Malek Garden is now much overgrown, although a few fallen columns, water rills, and steps in the undergrowth are a reminder of how it might have looked.

BAGH-E MOSTOUFI The walled Mostoufi Garden, in the village of Vanak on the slopes above Tehran, was laid out in the 1930s.

FARMANIEH An avenue of tall plane trees flanks the flowerbeds that frame the façade of the Italian ambassador's residence, built in the 19th century.

SA'DABAD PALACE Built in the Qajar period, the palace was used by Muhammad Reza, the last Pahlavi Shah, as a year-round residence after a failed assassination attempt. It stands in a park above Tajrish in what are now the northern suburbs of the city. Except for alleys of plane trees and some water channels and pools in the woods, the garden, with a large pool and fountain, has European characteristics with specimen magnolias and photinias set in an emerald lawn. The garden and the white palace, with French furniture and relics of the Pahlavis, are open to the public.

NATIONAL BOTANIC GARDEN OF IRAN The Botanic Garden (now the Research Institute of Forests and Rangelands), near the village of Karaj, 13 miles west of Tehran, was established in the 1970s, at the instigation of the Department of Conservation and, in particular, that of Eskander Firouz. The site was flat, stony, and windy, the soil pH high, and the climate extreme: summer temperatures often exceed 120°F, dropping to sub-zero in winter, and annual rainfall is 7 inches, none falling in summer. Trees were established as shelter belts, and ample water was provided by artesian wells and reservoirs created in the Alborz.

Edward Hyams, an expert on the design and function of botanic gardens, was called in as an adviser and to prepare a master plan. The design paid homage to the classic Persian garden, with the main avenues meeting in 17th-century Safavid style. Further radiating walks defining separate regions were planted to represent the natural plantscape of Iran's geographical areas:

The Caspian; the Zagros; the Alborz; and the deserts. Other areas were devoted to plants that flourish in highly alkaline conditions and summer heat.

Princess Fatima, sister of Mohammad Reza Shah, encouraged the building of a large rock garden. Will Ingwersen, an alpine rock garden expert and owner of a famous nursery in Sussex, England, constructed a semi-circular cliff face, 33 feet wide and 69 feet high, over which water, circulated by pumps, cascaded to a lake. Areas of rock planting were created with especially prepared soil pockets.

Ana Ala, English sister-in-law of Eskander Firouz, was responsible for a wild bulb collection and the library.

The garden can be visited by appointment, the trees and shrubs planted to represent the Caspian region being particularly relevant to Western gardeners. There are also an herbarium and scientific laboratories for the study of plant life, and a school of horticulture.

Kashan: Province of Isfahan

Kashan is an ancient oasis town on the site of the prehistoric city of Sialk. The Friday Mosque, much restored over centuries, dates to Seljuk times. The town has always been noted for its ceramics, silks, and carpets, and for Kashan roses (*Rosa × centifolia*), grown for rose water in the Mahallat Valley. Chardin described the caravanserai built by Shah 'Abbas I as the "first in all Persia." The tomb of Shah 'Abbas is a modest affair in the town. By the 19th century, the royal palace in its grounds, built when the Shah expanded the Bagh-e Fin, could be used as an inn by important travelers. Kashan was once notorious for a vicious black scorpion which, however, did not attack strangers.

BAGH-E FIN The approach to the Bagh-e Fin is along a shady avenue from the town of Kashan. The quadripartite garden (*see pages 94–7*), lying 4 miles to the southwest of the town, is one of the most beautiful in Persia, indeed holding its own among the great gardens of the world. Ample water, brought by *qanat* from the mountains and stored in a great cistern above the garden, still works by gravity to bubble through turquoise-tiled channels between ancient cypresses, which may have been planted in the 16th century, dating to the first mention of a walled enclosure where the Shah Isma'il Safavi was entertained by nobles. Shah 'Abbas developed a royal residence, bathhouses, and a central pavilion in the 17th century. The buildings were restored and used by Fath 'Ali Shah in the early 19th century. The bathhouse where the vizier Mirza Taqi Khan was murdered by order of the twenty-year-old Naser ad-Din Shah in 1852 can also be visited .

BORUJERDI HOUSE AND TABATABA'I HOUSE

These merchants' mansions in the southern part of the town of Kashan were built in

Isfahan: 'Abbasi Hotel Garden

the 19th century. Their gardens (with flowerbeds that await restoration) are within, hidden behind high walls. The Borujerdi House (Khaneh-ye Borujerdiha) is distinguished by six-sided *badgirs*. Throughout the buildings elaborate plasterwork portrays flowers and birds. The Tabataba'i House has two inner courtyards and central pools. The windows of the rooms are decorated with colored glass typical of the Qajar period. The northern section of Borujerdi House is still owned by one of the grandchildren of Borujerdi, but both mansions have been restored by the province and are open to the public.

Isfahan: Province of Isfahan

Gardens were made in Isfahan by the 10th-century Buyids, but the town's reputation as a garden city dates from the end of the 16th century when it became the Safavid capital under Shah 'Abbas. To the northeast is the ancient Friday Mosque, a mosaic of different periods. Many of the Safavid buildings, both religious and secular, including the storied bridges, have survived, although Lord Curzon writing in 1892 called the city "a wreck of fallen palaces." The few gardens that remain are shadows of their 17th-century glory, when they were the setting for receptions and festive scenes, but they are peaceful havens in the city center. Shaded by avenues of elm and Asian planes, they are planted with modern roses and some shrubs, dominated by yellow forsythia and purple-leaved Japanese berberis.

'ABBASI HOTEL GARDEN Originally a caravanserai next to the Madraseh-ye Madar-e Shah (Madraseh of the Shah's Mother, now known as the Madraseh-ye

Chahar Bagh), constructed to provide financial support to the *madraseh*, this is now a luxury hotel. The rooms look out from the two-storied arcade into the old courtyard, attractively gardened and full of flowers and scent. In traditional Persian style, the garden is divided into four, with a long central pool edged with poplars. From the garden there is a spectacular view of the blue-tiled dome of the neighboring 18th-century *madraseh*.

GARDEN OF THE MADRASEH-YE CHAHAR BAGH With entrance forbidden to women, the outer gate to the Madraseh of the Shah's Mother on the Chahar Bagh Avenue, built between 1704 and 1714, is one of the loveliest Safavid buildings in Isfahan. It has a richly decorated stalactite vault and wooden doors covered with floral motifs and inscriptions from the Koran. Unlike the courtyards of mosques, which are kept as empty spaces for prayer around a central ablution pool, the teaching academy has internal yards shaded with tall plane trees, surrounded by two-storied arches in which students work. In the main yard the buildings and trees are romantically reflected in a wide pool.

CHEHEL SOTUN Built in the 17th century in the new center of the city and aligned with the *maidan*—the main square created by Shah 'Abbas—the Chehel Sotun gets its name from the twenty plane tree columns, doubled to forty by reflection in the large water tank, which support the roof of the *talar* of the palace. Built for receptions and for entertaining rather than as a royal residence, the palace was originally set in a part of the park which stretched out behind the 'Ali Qapu Palace to the Chahar

Bagh Avenue. The pavilion, built between 1642 and 1662 during the reign of 'Abbas II, has mirrored walls that reflect the columns and avenues of elms and plane trees in the garden. Today, shrubs and modern roses are planted in the beds flanking the water tank. Open to the public.

HASHT BEHESHT The Palace of the Eight Paradises is just south of Imam Hosain Square in the park Shahid Raja'i (originally the Bagh-e Bolbol or Nightingale Garden). Built in 1669 by Shah Soleiman, the pleasure pavilion was renovated by Fath 'Ali Shah in the early 19th century. Today there are no nightingales to welcome lovers and few plane trees remain, but elms (*Ulmus minor*), still untouched by disease, line the lateral avenues. Although the water rills around the pavilion are dry and modern planting (and unsightly lamps) has dimmed its charms, the garden has trees and a pool with fountains which make it inviting. The octagonal building is one of the most beautiful pavilions in Isfahan. The floral frescoes decorating the inner walls and the magnificent stucco *muqarnas* vault are in good repair. Open to the public.

MAIDAN-E SHAH Of the original water features, including a channel which ran around the inside of the square, only a rectangular central pool remains. The two-storied arched buildings enclosing the central space, with stores on the ground floor, still stand, together with the principal buildings that formed part of Shah 'Abbas's great design. The 'Ali Qapu Pavilion lies in the center of the western side, the Mosque of Sheikh Lotfollah on the east, the superb entrance to the Bazar Qaisarieh (Imperial Bazaar) to the north, and the Imam Mosque, originally the Masjed-e Shah, to

the south. The square is treeless and burning hot in summer, but plans exist for its restoration.

CHAHAR BAGH AVENUE Today the Chahar Bagh leading down to the Zayandeh Rud and the thirty-three-arched Allahverdi Khan bridge, part of Shah 'Abbas's 17th-century complex, is a busy road lined with modern store façades but, shaded by plane trees and elms watered by *jubs*, enough remains to evoke the romance of earlier eras.

Natanz: the Friday Mosque

Natanz: Province of Isfahan

From Kashan, the road to Isfahan goes to Natanz where Shah 'Abbas is said to have slept under the plane tree by the 14th-century Friday Mosque, which is part of the funerary complex of a disciple of Sheikh Abu Sa'id, who died in 1049. According to legend, the three Magi came from Natanz.

Shiraz: Province of Fars

The main avenue was constructed in the 17th century to resemble the Chahar Bagh in Isfahan. After various political vicissitudes, Karim Khan Zand restored the city's prosperity and inaugurated a period of rebuilding in the 18th century. He built the bazaar (Bazar-e Vakil), with distinguished vaulted brick ceilings, and the Vakil Mosque, with floral tiling mostly of the Qajar period. Shiraz suffered from severe flooding in the last half of the 17th century and earthquakes in the early 19th further damaged buildings and gardens. Later in the 19th century, gardens of much earlier origins were restored and "improved." Modern Shiraz is a maze of classic courtyard houses, their rooms and gardens hidden behind high walls. Besides the traditional roses, Judas trees, scented orange groves, and cypresses, they are today enlivened by exotic introductions such as the Chinese Banksian rose and wisteria, salvias from Mexico, and scarlet flax, which thrive in the Shiraz microclimate. Scented stocks in the pale-colored terracotta pots found all over the country are arranged in patterns by the gardeners. Once famed for its vineyards, it still produces Syrah grapes for dried fruit.

BAGH-E DELGOSHA Lying to the northeast of the main avenue, the Garden of Heart's Ease may date to the 11th-century Seljuk period. It was restored by Karim Khan Zand, but came into the possession of a member of the Qavam al-Mulk family (now known as the Qavam-Shirazi) in 1845, who used the Bagh-e Delgosha as a winter residence. A central water channel leads to a 19th-century pavilion, flanked by orange trees, pomegranates, date palms, bushes of double yellow jasmine, walnut trees, and weeping mulberries. Open to the public.

BAGH-E ERAM The University Botanic Garden to the northwest of Shiraz is a 19th-century garden laid out before a 19th-century pavilion, but its layout of large reflecting pool and four waterways almost certainly owes its origins to an earlier era. It was owned originally by the Il-Khanis, or paramount tribal leaders of the Qashqa'i. The Qajar palace, the Kakh-e Eram, was a guesthouse for the Pahlavi shahs. To a plantsman it is the most interesting garden in Persia, with a great variety of traditional as well as introduced plants, and part of the garden is arranged for their display, while the traditional water channels and cross-axial rills and pathways remain. In spring, flowering Judas trees predominate among lilacs, palm trees, pomegranates, koelreuterias, and photinias (most labels are in Latin). At the entrance there are flowerpots filled with scented stocks. In the lower garden a great cypress alley shades orange groves. Open to the public.

Shiraz: Bagh-e Delgosha

BAGH-E GOLSHAN The Flower Garden, or 'Afifabad, was constructed in 1863 by Qavam al-Mulk Mirza 'Ali Mohammad Khan, head of the Qavam-Shirazi family. Its austere pavilion, reached by steep steps to the east, looks over a large square pool on its south side, where cypress avenues provide shade. Also in the grounds are the remains of a Turkish bathhouse and a small teahouse. To the east a linear pool has been restored with flowerbed planting. Now an army museum, the garden has a neglected air. Open to the public.

HAFEZ'S TOMB GARDEN

Aramgah-e Hafez, on the north bank of the river opposite Melli Park, has shaded pools and beautiful gardens surrounding the mausoleum—a small open pavilion. Pale terracotta pots, set in ranks, are filled with scented stocks in spring. Since the middle of the 15th century the mausoleum has been a place of pilgrimage for people coming to glean advice from the poet's writings. After the Koran, Hafez's *Divan* is still more widely read in Persia than any other literature. The tomb has been heavily restored and enlarged in the last two centuries. In 1952 the last Pahlavi Shah added a Western-style classical building. An adjacent teahouse provides a resting-place. Open to the public.

BAGH-E KHALILI Built during the early part of the reign of Reza Shah Pahlavi in the 20th century, the garden is noted for its collection of rare plants, assembled around a series of pools. Open to the public.

NARANJESTAN (BAGH-E QAVAM) Begun in the 1870s, the garden and buildings we see today are part of the original *biruni*, used for business and entertaining.

Shiraz: Bagh-e Nazar

Built as a town house for the Qavam family, the grand *talar* (reception hall), decorated with mirrors and colored glass, looks out to an elaborate patterned water garden, the layout of rills and wider pools lying between flowerbeds filled with roses and perennials. An avenue of tall date palms gives shade and is flanked by orange groves. The harem and private buildings are inaccessible.

BAGH-E NAZAR Now the Fars Museum (Muze-ye Pars), the 18th-century mausoleum of Karim Khan Zand was despoiled by the vengeful Agha Mohammad Khan, the first Qajar ruler. Now restored, the octagonal building has a tiled façade including depictions of flowers, birds, hunting scenes and legendary romantic tales from the Persian poets. The garden, originally much larger, has a rectangular central pool and quantities of bright and scented flowers in the attractive pale terracotta pots seen everywhere in Iran. Open to the public.

BAGH-E NOU Sa'di's tomb (Aramgah-e Sa'di) lies in the northeastern suburbs of Shiraz, within walking distance of that of Hafez. It was restored by Karim Khan but embellished by Mohammad Reza Shah with a new Western-style classical building. A grove of tall dark cypresses towers over the mausoleum, constructed in 1948, which is less visited than than that of Hafez. The interior walls bear tilework and panels inscribed with quotations from the poet's work. Water from a *qanat* passes through an octagonal pool full of black and gold fish. The garden, in many ways a repetition of planting seen at Hafez's Tomb Garden, somehow lacks the instinctive charm that the Hafez gardeners achieve. Open to the public.

BAGH-E TAKHT The terraced Throne Garden may date to the Safavid period but has been obscured by modern building.

Persepolis (Takht-e Jamshid): Province of Fars

The name Tahkt-e Jamshid (the Throne of Jamshid) is a reference to Ferdousi's *Shahnameh*. First excavations of the ruined city were made in the 19th century.

APADANA PALACE It seems more than likely that the Achaemenid kings made garden courtyards connected to their private dwellings at the great Palace of Persepolis, but archaeologists cannot be certain. An obvious site is a sunken yard below the Hadish, the palace of Xerxes, reached by a steep stairway. Reconstructions of the whole complex show that this area was almost certainly planted with shade trees and flowers.

NAQSH-E ROSTAM About 2½ miles north of Persepolis, a Zoroastrian fire temple from Achaemenian times stands at the base of the cliff where the tombs of Darius and his three successors were cut in the rock face. Eight bas-reliefs, carved in the cliff face at a later date, include depictions of the Sasanian Ardeshir I and the god Ahura Mazda, and the captured Roman Emperor Valerian.

Pasargadae: Province of Fars

The ruins are dispersed over a wide area across the Murghab Plain, about 45 miles from Persepolis.

CYRUS THE GREAT'S GARDEN The ruins of Cyrus's palace stand on the plain. The ancient stone-dressed watercourses, a pattern of narrow channels opening out into square basins, can still be seen. Open to the public.

CYRUS THE GREAT'S TOMB Originally in the royal park at Pasargadae, the tomb of Alexander the Great's hero, built south of the palace in about 530 BC, is a simple and awe-inspiring sight. After the introduction of the Islamic faith it was called the Shrine of Solomon's Mother, and a *mehrab* was carved inside the building to face Mecca. Nothing remains of the *pairidaeza* that surrounded the tomb but willows still give shade to picnicking tourists.

FIRUZABAD The ruins of the Sasanian palace at Firuzabad, south of Shiraz, once surrounded by a verdant oasis, include the arched *ayvan* overlooking a pool, which is the remains of the original formal garden.

Yazd: Province of Yazd

The town of Yazd, completely surrounded by desert, is reputed to have the hottest summers in Persia. With Kerman, it is one of the last strongholds of Zoroastrianism and on the hills outside the town stand the remains of the towers of silence which they used for funerary purposes. In the town a modern temple, where the sacred fire is kept burning, displays the winged symbol of Azura Mazda. Narrow streets wind between mud walls and domed houses, the skyline enlivened by *badgir* which cool the lower rooms in summer. The Friday Mosque was founded in the 12th century but partially rebuilt between 1334 and 1365.

BAGH-E DOULATABAD This 18th-century garden is divided into a ceremonial reception area and a private space. A winter pavilion faces south down a long avenue flanked by pines and cypresses, while a summer house, shaded by cypresses and cooled by a tall windtower, faces north. Water is brought by *qanats*. Pomegranate orchards, cherry trees, and shade-giving cypresses thrive, watered by earthenware jars buried at the roots and kept filled. The garden is under restoration, a shadow of its 18th-century self, but the summer pavilion, with colored glass and interior pools cooled by the magnificent windtower, is well worth a visit. Open to the public.

Tabas: Province of Yazd

Oranges and lemons flourish in the milder winters in this oasis town, the climate being closer to that of the garden city of Shiraz than of the towns of the higher plateau. Situated almost exactly between the Dasht-e Kavir and Dasht-e Lut, Tabas is a seven hours' drive from Mashad and the remotest

town of its size in all Iran. It was important as a trade route and was embellished in the 18th century during the reign of Nader Shah, although its major monuments, including a mosque, windtowers, and older houses, were almost completely destroyed in an earthquake of 1978. Today the town, composed of modern flat-roofed houses, is undistinguished, but the mild climate, ample water supply, and thriving garden should make it a popular winter resort.

BAGH-E GOLSHAN This garden, in Persia ranking second only to the Bagh-e Fin in Kashan, survived the earthquake of 1978 almost intact, losing only the 18th-century governor's house which was aligned with the central water feature. It is an excellent example of a traditional Islamic paradise garden and is of considerable interest to historians and plantsmen. Rushing water fed from springs, at 45 gallons per second, provides the tumbling cascades with the power to fill the 20-acre enclosure with

Mahan: vineyard

constant sound. Plants thrive in the beneficial microclimate: stately date palms and cypresses are linked with gray-leaved *Populus euphratica*, and Judas trees, eucalypts, jasmine, and citrus groves mingle with roses, cycads, pomegranates, hollyhocks, and poppies. The garden, obviously the pride of a team of gardeners who constantly spray the paved walks to keep the dust down and to cool the air, is immaculately maintained as the center of town life. Open to the public.

Mahan: Province of Kerman

The small but prosperous town of Mahan is a green oasis, flanked by snow-capped mountains, 26 miles southeast of Kerman. It is a town of citrus and pomegranate orchards, whose roads are lined with tamarisks and oleanders and shaded by eucalyptus and cypresses, with areas where grapevines are grown on pillars made from baked mud. Since the 15th century, the mausoleum of Shah Ne'matollah Vali (d.1431) has made Mahan a place of pilgrimage. A further attraction is the 19th-century garden of Shahzadeh, a few miles toward the mountains to the southeast.

MAUSOLEUM OF NE'MATOLLAH VALI Aramgah-e Shah Ne'matollah Vali, the mausoleum of the Sufi divine and poet, was described by Sir Roger Stevens as comprising "the most ravishing single group of buildings in Iran." Features of the shrine complex were constructed at different periods. The turquoise-tiled dome dates to 1436 when Ahmad-Shah Dakani, a king of the Deccan Bahmaniyeh dynasty in India, began the building. It was enlarged during the reign of Shah 'Abbas I and Qajar minarets were added in the 1840s. A series of courtyards or garden enclosures is traversed before reaching the grave, each dominated by tall cypresses shading pools, which keep the air cool and serve for ablutions; beds of flowers and potted geraniums edge the water. The whole place is in perfect harmony: elegant tiled gateways, placid cooling pools, and greenery make this a paradise for the traveler.

BAGH-E SHAHZADEH The beautiful Prince's Garden, south of the pilgrimage city of Mahan, is also known as Farman Farma's Garden, named after the brother of the Governor of Kerman who built it in the 1880s. Water from the mountains is still stored in a vast cistern outside the walls. A gate in the walled enclosure leads to the ruins of the summer pavilion, from which there is a view of the cascading waterway and the governor's residence, now a restaurant, against a backdrop of snow-capped mountains. Cypresses and willows overhang the flowerbeds planted with modern roses. In the orchards on either side of the terraces, picnickers spread their carpets on the rough grass and brew *chai* (tea) in the shade. Open to the public.

Damghan: Province of Semnan

The original capital of the Parthians on the main trade route between Asia and the west, Damghan is distinguished by its early mosque, known by some as Tarikh Khaneh (Dark House) and by others as Tari Khaneh (God's House), built in 'Abbasid times between 750 and 789. It is set beside an 11th-century minaret and a round tower, the Aramgah-e Pir 'Alamdar, dating to 1026, both with interesting brick patterns. The city was destroyed by the Mongols in the 13th century.

Tus: Ferdousi Mausoleum

CHESHMEH-E 'ALI The gardens of Cheshmeh-e 'Ali ('Ali's Spring) lie in a well-watered valley in the foothills of the southern Alborz, 17 miles north of the town of Damghan. Fath 'Ali Shah, who was born at Damghan, formalized the water and built a hunting pavilion on an island in its midst. Although the garden was used by the reigning shah until the end of the 19th century, the buildings are romantic ruins.

Tus: Province of Khorasan

Tus, the birthplace of the poet Ferdousi, born *c.*940, was the capital of the region before nearby Mashad grew up around the bones of the Imam Reza. An earlier honey-colored 12th-century Seljuk mausoleum is surrounded by attractive gardens.

FERDOUSI MAUSOLEUM The plans for the mausoleum celebrating the thousandth anniversary of Ferdousi's death in *c.*1033 included a simple cenotaph standing on a broad flight of steps around a square cone in white stone, surrounded by appro-

priate Persian-style gardens. However, by order of Reza Shah, this concept was abandoned a year later for a more monumental building which was erected in its stead. Decorated with huge bulls' heads copied from the columns of Persepolis, steep staircases lead up to the interior of the mausoleum. The most impressive part of the monument is the basement where vast modern bas-reliefs depict stories from the *Shahnameh.* A porter/ticket collector will give a dramatic display, declaiming verses from Ferdousi's works in front of a relevant carving. The garden could be attractive with colorful flowerbeds but, with railings enclosing the pool, it has a distinctly municipal air. Open to the public.

The Caspian Shore: Province of Mazanderan

Naturally high precipitation occurs in the province of Mazanderan (although the southeastern shore of the Caspian is much drier than further west in Gilan). Little remains of the gardens laid out in the 17th century by Shah 'Abbas in a series of separate but connected *chahar bagh* enclosures on different levels, with central water cascades and each with its own pavilion and audience halls. Within a hundred years, the gardens and those of nearby Farahabad were destroyed by invading Cossacks and Turkomen from the east, the rest gradually overtaken by building and neglect. At Ashraf (modern Behshahr), the Safavid gardens had eight distinct areas, at least one of which was the private palace of the Shah and another, the Bagh-e Haram, was reserved for the women of the harem. A villa perched on a wooded hill a few miles to the west gave views to the sea and was embellished by Shah Safi I twenty years

Ramsar: Caspian Palace

later, but is now out of bounds as a military installation. The resort town of Ramsar in western Mazanderan has a large 20th-century hotel with an elaborately gardened esplanade avenue stretching down to the Caspian shore.

ASHRAF The only garden which remains of those made by Shah 'Abbas, so well described by travelers, is now the public garden in the bustling town of Behshahr, a large walled expanse where water cascades down two narrow channels, hemmed in by tall cypresses and orange groves. Situated under the slopes of the northern foothills of the Alborz, it is well supplied with water from the mountains. Exotics, such as the yellow Banksian rose, *Rosa chinensis* "Old Blush," plumbago, mimosa, pittosporum, and topiarized euonymus, reflect modern gardening influences, but the garden retains much of the atmosphere of a *chahar bagh*. The ancient cypresses, 26 feet high, box trees, and huge pomegranates—native on

the mountain slopes above—might almost date to the garden's inception. Most of the Safavid complex has disappeared, but the garden seems resilient and is well maintained, only slightly marred by an excess of blue and white paintwork.

BABOL The Qajar palace, dating to about 1900, is a white chocolate-box affair, set in 7,170 acres, and was used by Reza Shah as a summer residence. Today it is part of a medical school, but the garden has remnants of interesting planting. Orange groves, magnolias, wisteria, and Banksian roses, hemmed in by box hedges, and a splendid dark tunnel of bay (*Laurus nobilis*) survive to demonstrate the favorable gardening climate.

CASPIAN PALACE The Caspian Palace and its gardens, built by the Pahlavis and lived in by Mohammad Reza Shah and his family until the revolution of 1979, is set in the wooded foothills at Ramsar, with superlative views northward over the Caspian. There is no hint of the traditional Persian garden and the white palace is now a museum. The gardens are well kept and include remarkable trees; two Norfolk Island pines (*Araucaria heterophylla*) and a large *Pinus roxburghii* grow near the palace among a French-style parterre pattern of box.

Tabriz: Province of East Azerbaijan

During his travels between 1325 and 1354 Ibn Battuta visited Tabriz at the height of its importance as an *entrepot* between China and Europe. He describes the mosque—its remains now part of the *arg* (citadel)—with a court paved with marble and walls

faced with tiles, traversed by a canal of water, containing all sorts of trees, vines, and jasmines. Tabriz is now the capital of East Azerbaijan.

SHAH-GOLI Tradition assigns this grand garden to the late 18th century but it seems possible that Shah-Goli (also known as Shah Gol) was constructed earlier —some suggest even in the 14th century — and then restored and the high terraces added in the 19th century. It is situated 4 miles to the southeast of Tabriz. Its main feature is a huge artificial square lake (670 feet), the northern side of which was built up by immense earth moving. From the top of the slope, the lake appears to float over the valley. A causeway leads out to an octagonal pavilion (today a pleasant restaurant), which was once crowned with a dome. The high terraces are fed from a spring and water descends in five cascades backed by tall poplars. Splendidly romantic in photographs taken at the height of summer, the Shah-Goli is disappointing if visited when the surrounding trees and orchards are not in leaf, the bare boughs revealing various cabins and the suburbs of Tabriz set around the garden.

Tabriz: Shah-Goli

FATHABAD Near to the Shah-Goli but easily missed is the garden of Fathabad, its central water canal almost hidden among lush orchards. The long water axis follows several changes of level and widens out below the house into a square pool surrounded by massive and ancient trees. A modern house has replaced the original pavilion.

GANJEHEZADEH'S HOUSE, BEHNAM'S HOUSE AND QADAKI HOUSE In 1994 the Sahand Industrial University in Tabriz acquired several almost adjacent old houses in the Maqsudiyeh neighborhood of the city, and has restored them and their courtyard gardens under the auspices of the Cultural Heritage Office of East Azerbaijan province. Some areas serve as classrooms and reception rooms for students of the Islamic Art University of Tabriz. They are open to the public on Thursdays and Fridays and by previous arrangement.

CONSTITUTION HOUSE Built in 1868, the house was recently restored as a museum. It was used as a meeting place before the Constitutional Revolution at the beginning of the 20th century. The main façade looks out on a pool and garden.

Ardabil: Province of Ardabil

Once an important Sufi center, Ardabil is the place of origin of the Safavid rulers. Although the famous Ardabil carpet in the Victoria and Albert Museum in London, woven between 1539 and 1540, is decorated with scattered flowers, it does not have a garden theme.

SHRINE OF SHEIKH SAFI AD-DIN Sheikh Safi ad-Din (1252–1334) was an ancestor of Shah Isma'il, who is buried in the same tomb. In the early 17th century Shah 'Abbas had a garden constructed

Qazvin: Chehel Sotun

around one of the tombs, at the same time as he revamped the Chini Khaneh (China Chamber) in order to display his Chinese porcelains and celadon wares (some of which are now in the Tehran Museum), with which he endowed the shrine. In 1828 the Russians looted valuable Persian books and rare manuscripts that, today, form the core of the St Petersburg National Library Oriental Collection.

Soltanieh: Province of Zanjan

At the site of Soltanieh near Zanjan, where the magnificent early-14th-century mausoleum of Sultan Oljaitu is being restored, quartered gardens are being laid out within the curtilage of its walled enclosure.

Qazvin: Province of Qazvin

Qazvin, surrounded by vineyards and orchards, has a Seljuk mosque and buildings constructed during the time of the Safavid

Shah Tahmasp, when the town became the capital of Persia. Little remains of the original palace and garden complex, or of the great square used for polo and receptions, laid out in the 16th century (see Chapter 6). At the heart of the city is the site of the old royal gardens, faced by the gateway of 'Ali Qapu, similar to an *ayvan* of a Safavid mosque.

CHEHEL SOTUN The only building of remaining interest in Qazvin is a pavilion of the royal garden, which, with an extra story, wooden balconies, and Qajar-type windows added in 1840, now stands in a small park, with attractive planting and pools. Originally reserved for the women of the harem, this is now a museum.

Behestun: Province of Kermanshah

The famous rock relief of Darius I at Behestun, cut to commemorate his victory over Magnus Gaumata in 520 BC, is worth a visit and this can be combined with the Sasanian grottoes of Taq-e Bostan.

TAQ-E BOSTAN The Taq-e Bostan is one of the few remaining examples of Sasanian work. Two grottoes with rock carvings overlook a large pool and pleasant garden. A lower panel represents Khosrou II, a contemporary of the Prophet Mohammad and the last Sasanian emperor, flanked by the Zoroastrian gods Ahura Mazda and Anahita. The entrance is decorated with floral motifs, with two winged figures holding a crown, and the inner walls with hunting scenes. The right-hand "cave" shows Shapur II and Shapur III leaning on their swords, with inscriptions in Old Persian.

Royal houses of Persia, with principal rulers and conquests

ACHAEMENIANS 558–331 BC
  Cyrus the Great 558–528 BC
  Cambyses 528–522 BC
  Darius I 521–485 BC
  Xerxes I 485–465 BC
  Artaxerxes 465–425 BC
  Darius III 336–333 BC
ALEXANDER THE GREAT
  (336–323 BC) CONQUEST
  OF PERSIA 333 BC
SELEUCIDS 323–223 BC
PARTHIANS 223 BC–AD 226
SASANIANS AD 224–642
  Ardeshir I 226–40
  Shapur I 242–71
  Shapur II 310–79
  Khosrou I 531–79
  Khosrou II Parvis 591–628
ISLAMIC INVASION 642
  Umayyad Caliphs,
    Damascus 661–750
  'Abbasid Caliphs, Baghdad
    and Samarra 762–1258
MINOR DYNASTIES
  642–1047
  Taherids 821–73
  Saffarids 867–903
  Samanids 892–999
  Buyids 945–1055
  Ghaznavids 977–1186
SELJUKS 1051–1157
  Toghrel Beg 1055–63
  Alp Ardan 1063–72
  Malek Shah 1072–92
  Soltan Sanjar 1096–1157
FIRST MONGOL INVASION
  1220–27
  Genghiz Khan 1206–27
SECOND MONGOL INVASION
  1251–56

ILKHANIDS 1270–35
  Hulagu Khan 1256–65
  Abaqa 1265–81
  Ghazan Khan 1295–1304
  Oljaitu 1304–16
  Abu Sa'id 1317–35
TIMURIDS 1370–1500
  Timur (Samarkand)
    1370–1405
  Shah Rokh (Herat) 1408–47
  Ulogh Beg 1447–49
SAFAVIDS 1502–1736
  Shah Isma'il Safavi 1502–24
  Shah Tahmasp 1524–76
  Shah 'Abbas I 1587–1629
  Shah Safi I 1629–41
  Shah 'Abbas II 1641–66
  Shah Safi II (Soleiman) 1666
    (1668)–1694
  Soltan Hosain 1694–1722
  Tahmasp II 1722–32
  'Abbas III 1732–36
THE INTERREGNUM 1736–94
  Nader Shah 1736–47
  Karim Khan Zand 1759–79
QAJARS 1787–1925
  Agha Mohammad Khan
    1796–97
  Fath 'Ali Shah 1797–1834
  Mohammad Shah 1834–48
  Naser ad-Din Shah 1848–96
  Mozaffar ad-Din Shah
    1896–1907
  Mohammad 'Ali Shah
    1907–09
  Soltan Ahmad Shah 1909–25
PAHLAVIS
  Reza Shah Pahlavi 1925–40
  Mohammad Reza Shah
    1941–79
ISLAMIC REPUBLIC 1979–

Glossary of Persian terms

ab water
abad settlement
ab-pakhshan sluice
a'ineh-kari mirrorwork
andaruni domestic part of
  house
aqa title used for a man
arg citadel
ashjar grove
ashura 10th day of Muharran,
  day of mourning for the
  martyrdom of Hosein, the
  son of 'Ali and grandson of
  Mohammad, killed at
  Karbala
'atr rose essence
ayvan barrel-vaulted half-
  sphere used as an entry
  portal or to face onto
  a courtyard
bab door, chapter
badgir windtower
badiya nomadic encampment
bagh garden
baghban gardener
bagh-eram Garden of Paradise
  in the Koran
bahar spring
bait house or living apartment
bazar market
behesht paradise
biruni male part of a house
bolbol nightingale
bolbolistan garden favored by
  a nightingale
bostan orchard or garden
caravanserai inn for travelers
  and their animals
chadar carved water screen
  (India)

chahar bagh garden divided into quadrants

chai tea

chehel sotun forty pillars

dargah formal portal

divan office of administration of government, collection of a poet's works

divan-i 'amm public audience hall

divan-i khass private audience hall

divankhaneh court of justice

fal omen

farah joy

farangi foreigner ("Frank")

farsakh unit of length

favareh fountain jet

ferdous paradise

garmsir warm area ("land of palms")

ghazal verse form of five to twelve lines

gol rose or any flower

golab rose water

golbang song of the nightingale

golbon rose bush

golestan flower/rose garden

Golestan The Rose Garden, collected anecdotes and poems by Sa'di

golnar pomegranate flower

gombad dome

guebre Zoroastrian

hadith Traditions of the Prophet Mohammad, second only in importance to the Koran as Muslim holy writings

hajj pilgrimage to Mecca

hammam public or communal baths

haram sanctuary ("forbidden")

haramsarai harem (women's quarters)

hasht behesht eight paradises – name often given to octagonal pavilions

hejri Islamic dating system starting in AD 622 (the Prophet Muhammad's emigration from Mecca to Medina

hookah water pipe for smoking, see *qalyan*

houz-khaneh pool house

imam prayer leader; in a Shiite context an infallible divinely guided leader

ivan see *ayvan*

jannat Muslim celestial garden

jarib unit of land measurement, approximately 2½ acres

jehad holy war ("struggle to reform")

jub open water channel

kakh palace or castle

kariz see *qanat*

khal'at embroidered robe of honor

khalifa caliph ("successor")

Khamseh Five Tales, collection of poems by Nezami

khan lodging place for travelers and merchants

Khan honorific title

khaneh chamber

khanom title for a woman

khata'i flowerheads and palmettes used in decoration (from Khotan in East Turkistan)

kilim/gelim coarse woven floor covering in tapestry weave

kolah headwear

kufic Arabic script with squared letters

lalehzar garden of tulips

madi canal system

madina city

madraseh Muslim religious college

maidan large open square, ceremonial open space

malqaf air-shaft or wind catcher

mashad mausoleum of a martyr

masjed mosque ("place of prostration")

me'mar architect

mehrab arched niche indicating the direction of Mecca for prayer

menbar pulpit in Friday mosques

mirab controller of water ("water prince")

mirza prefix signifying a secretary or scribe; suffix (Timurid) signifying prince

mojtahid cleric trained in theology to a high level

mollah-bashi chief cleric

mollah cleric trained in theology

moqarnas honeycomb or stalactite decoration in domes and arches formed by squinches

mostoufi accountant/treasurer

nabat plant in general

Nou Ruz spring equinox – Persian New Year

padishah emperor

pairidaeza paradise garden

pishtaq lofty arch framing an *ayvan*

qaisariyya royal bazaar

qalyan hubble-bubble pipe

qanat underground water channel originating in the mountains (*kariz* also used)

qasr palace, residence

qebla direction of Mecca, to which Muslims face when praying

revaq arcaded court

robat caravanserai

sahn courtyard

sardab underground room for summer use

sardsir cold area

shadarvan carved water screen (*chadar* in India)

shahanshah "King of Kings" (Malik al-Moluk)

Shahnameh Book of Kings by Ferdausi, the Persian national epic

shekufeh blossom

Shi'ites Muslims who believe the caliphate is hereditary; partisans of 'Ali and his descendants

simurgh mythical bird similar to the phoenix

squinch section in a vault which transfers the angle of two walls to make it possible to place a dome over a square

stele slab or column of stone bearing an inscription or carved image

stucco mold of carved plaster, often painted, used to decorate walls

sufi mystic

Sunnis followers of the Sunni branch of Islam, who chose Abu Bakr, the Prophet's closest companion, as his deputy

sura chapter of the Koran

taj crown or cap worn under a turban

takht throne

talar open hall or porch

toman unit of Iranian currency equivalent to 10 rials

tuba tree of paradise

vakil regent

vazir vizier or government minister

yailaq summer quarters of tribes

Persian plants

Latin name
Common name | *Persian name*

ACACIA FARNESIANA
acacia | *aqaqi*
ACER
maple | *adj, afra*
ACER PSEUDOPLATANUS
sycamore | *afra-ye bozorg*
ACER VELUTINUM
maple | *afra*
ALBIZIA JULIBRISSIN
silk tree | *derakht-e abrisham*
AMARANTHUS CAUDATUS
amaranthus, love-lies-bleeding | *bostan afruz*
ANEMONE
anemone | *shaqayiq-e nu'man*
Bamboo (various)
bamboo | *khaizaran*
ASTER
aster | *nina*
BUXUS SEMPERVIRENS
box | *shemshad*
CALENDULA
marigold | *hamisheh bahar, sahra'i, khojastih*
CARPINUS BETULUS
hornbeam | *alouch, mamraz*
CERATONIA SILIQUA
carob | *kharnub*
CERCIS SILIQUASTRUM
Judas tree | *arghavan*
CHEIRANTHUS
wallflower | *khairi*
CITRUS LIMON
lemon | *limu*
CITRUS MEDICA
citron | *turanj*
CITRUS SINENSIS
orange | *naranj*

CROCUS SATIVUS
saffron | *za'faran*
CUPRESSUS
cypress | *nashk, derakht*
CUPRESSUS SEMPERVIRENS
Italian cypress | *derakht-e sarv*
CYDONIA OBLONGA
quince | *beh*
DIOSPYROS EBENUM
ebony | *abnus*
DIOSPYROS KHAKI
persimmon | *khormalu*
ELAEAGNUS ANGUSTIFOLIA
Russian olive | *senjed*
FAGUS
beech | *zan, tcheler, maras*
FAGUS ORIENTALIS
beech | *rash*
FICUS
fig | *anjir*
FRAXINUS
ash | *zaban gondjeshk*
FRAXINUS ORNUS
F. ROTUNDIFOLIA
ash | *zaban*
HYACINTHUS
hyacinth | *sonbol*
INDIGOFERA TINCTORIA
indigo | *nil*
IRIS
iris | *zanbagh*
JASMINUM
jasmine | *yasaman, yasamin*
JUGLANS NIGRA
walnut | *gerdu*
JUNIPERUS
juniper | *avar, ors*
LILIUM
lily | *susan*
MALUS
apple | *sib*
MANDAGORA OFFICINARUM
mandrake | *mehrgiah*
MATTHIOLA
stock | *shab-bu*
MEDICAGO SATIVA
alfalfa, lucerne | *yunjeh*
MESPILUS GERMANICUS
medlar | *azgil*

MORUS
mulberry | *tut*
MORUS ALBA
white mulberry | *tut-e sefid*
MORUS ALBA 'Pendula'
weeping mulberry | *tut-e majnoon*
MORUS NIGRA
black mulberry | *shah tut*
MYOSOTIS
forget-me-not | *marzangush*
MYRTUS
myrtle | *murd*
NARCISSUS
narcissus | *narges*
NERIUM OLEANDER
oleander | *kharzahreh*
NICOTIANA
tobacco plant | *tutun*
NYMPHAEA/NELUMBO
lotus | *nilufar*
OCIMUM
basil | *shahasparam*
PAPAVER
poppy | *shaqayeq, khash khash*
PAPAVER SOMNIFERUM
opium poppy | *tariyak*
PARROTIA PERSICA
ironwood, Persian teakwood | *chub-e sakht*
PHOENIX DACTYLIFERA
date palm | *nakhl, khorma*
PHRAGMITES AUSTRALIS
reed | *nai*
PINUS
pine tree | *kaj, sanubar*
PISTACIA VERA
pistachio | *pesteh*
PLATANUS ORIENTALIS
plane tree | *chenar*
POPULUS ALBA
F. PYRAMIDALIS
white-stemmed poplar | *khadang*
POPULUS NIGRA ITALICA
Lombardy poplar | *tabrizi*
PRUNUS ARMENIACA
apricot | *zardalu*

PRUNUS AVIUM
bird cherry | *gilas*
PRUNUS CERASUS
sour cherry | *albalu*
PRUNUS DULCIS (formerly AMYGDALUS ARABICUS)
almond | *badam*
PRUNUS PERSICA
peach | *holu*
PUNICA GRANATUM
pomegranate | *anar*
QUERCUS
oak | *balut*
RANUNCULUS
ranunculus | *alale*
ROSA BANKSIAE 'Lutea'
Banksian rose | *ashbar tala'i*
ROSA CANINA
dog rose | *nastaran*
ROSA
white rose | *nasrin*
ROSA FOETIDA
yellow rose | *gol-e zard*
SACCHARUM OFFICINARUM
sugarcane | *naishekar*
SALIX
willow | *bid*
SANTALUM
sandalwood | *sandal*
TAMARIX ORIENTALIS
tamarisk | *gaz-e nareng*
THYMUS
thyme | *sisanbar*
TILIA
lime tree/linden | *narmdar*
TRIFOLIUM
clover | *shabdar*
TULIPA
tulip | *laleh*
ULMUS MINOR
elm | *narvan*
VIOLA
violet | *banafsheh*
VITIS
grape | *angur*
ZIZIPHUS JUJUBA
jujube | *'onab*

Bibliography

BABUR *The Babur-nama in English* transl. A. S. Beveridge, London 1922

BELL, Gertrude *Persian Pictures*, London 1928

——*The Early Letters* edited by E. Richmond, London 1937

BERNIER, François *Travels in the Mogul Empire*, Oxford University Press 1914

BERNUS-TAYLOR, Marthe (ed) *Arabesques et Jardins de Paradis: Collections Français d'art Islamique* (exhibition catalogue), Louvre 1989

BINYON, Lawrence, J. V. S. Wilkinson and Basil Gray *Persian Miniature Painting*, Dover 1971

BLAIR, Sheila S., and Jonathan Bloom *The Art and Architecture of Islam 1250–1800*, Yale University Press 1994

BREND, Barbara *Islamic Art*, British Museum Press & Harvard University Press 1991

BROOKES, John *Gardens of Paradise*, Weidenfeld & Nicolson 1987

BROWNE, E.G. *A Year Amongst the Persians*, London 1893

BYRON, Robert *The Road to Oxiana*, Oxford University Press 1966

Cambridge History of Iran, Cambridge University Press 1968

CANBY, Sheila *The Golden Age of Persia 1501-1722* British Museum Press 1999

CHARDIN, Sir John *Voyages de chavalier Chardin en Perse, et autres lieux de l'Orient*, Louis de L'Orme 1711

CLARK, Emma *Underneath which Rivers Flow: the Symbolism of the Islamic Garden*, Prince of Wales Institute of Architecture 1997

COSTE, PASCAL *Monuments de la Perse, mesurés, dessinés, et décrits*, Paris 1867

COWELL, F. R. *The Garden as Fine Art*, Weidenfeld & Nicolson 1978

CROWE, Sylvia and Sheila Haywood *The Gardens of Mughal India*, Thames & Hudson 1972

CURZON, G. N. *Persia and the Persian Question*, London 1892

DANESHDUST, Ya'qub *Once There Was a Town Called Tabas*, Tehran 1990

DIXON HUNT, John (ed) *Garden History: Issues, Approaches, Methods: 'The Medieval Islamic Garden; typology and hydraulics'*, Yasser Tabbaa, Dumbarton Oaks 1992

FERRIER, R. W. *A Journey to Persia*, I. B. Tauris 1996

FITZGERALD, Edward (translator) *Rubaiyat of Omar Khayyam*, 1859

FLANDIN, Eugène, and Pascal Coste *Voyage en Perse 1840–1842*, Paris 1846–7

FOSTER, William *Sir Thomas Herbert's Travels in Persia 1627/9*, London 1928

FRASER, James B. *Travels and Adventures in the Persian Provinces on the Southern Banks of the Caspian Sea*, 1826

FRYE, Richard *The Golden Age of Persia*, Weidenfeld & Nicolson 1975

The Works of Mrs Gaskell Volume VII 'Cousin Phillis and other Tales', Smith Elder & Co 1906

GHAHREMAN, Ahmad *Flora of Iran* Volumes 1–20 (in Persian, English and French), Institute of Forests and Rangelands/ Tehran University 2000

GIBB, H. A. R. (ed) *The Travels of Ibn Battuta*, Munshiram Manoharlal 1999

GRAY, Basil *Persian Painting*, Bokking International 1995

HAJI-QASSEMI, Kambiz (ed) *Ganjnameh: Mansions of Kashan*, Iranian Cultural Organization 1996

Heavenly Art, Earthly Beauty (exhibition catalogue), Amsterdam 2000

HATTSTEIN, M., and P. Delius (eds) *Islam: Art and Architecture*, Konemann 2000

HEDIN, Sven *Overland to India*, Leipzig 1910

HERODOTUS *The Histories* transl. Aubrey de Selincourt, Penguin 1954

HILLENBRAND, Robert *Islamic Architecture*, Edinburgh University Press 1994

HOBHOUSE, Penelope *Plants in Garden History*, Pavilion 1992

—— *Gardening Through the Ages*, Simon & Schuster 1992

—— *The Story of Gardening*, Dorling Kindersley 2002

KHANSARI, Mehdi, M. Reza Moghtader and Minouch Yavari *The Persian Garden*, Washington 1998

JELLICOE, Geoffrey *The Landscape of Man*, Thames & Hudson 1975

JELLICOE, Geoffrey and Susan, Patrick Goode and Michael Lancaster (eds) *The Oxford Companion to Gardens*, Oxford University Press 1986

THE KORAN, transl. N. J. Dawood, Penguin 1956

LAMBTON, A. K. S. *The Persian Land Reform 1962–1966*, Clarendon Press 1969

LEHRMAN, Jonas *Earthly Paradise*, Thames & Hudson 1980

LE STRANGE, G. *Clavijo Embassy to Tamerlane*, Routledge 1928

MALCOLM, Sir John *Sketches of Persia*, John Murray 1828

MacDOUGALL, E. B., and R. Ettinghausen (eds) *The Islamic Garden*, Dumbarton Oaks 1976

MacDOUGALL, E. B., and Donald Wilber *Persian Gardens and Garden Pavilions*, Dumbarton Oaks 1979

MICHELL, George (ed) *Architecture of the Islamic World*, Thames & Hudson 1978

MOYNIHAN, Elizabeth *Paradise as a Garden in Persia and Mughal India*, Brazilier 1979

NICOLSON, Harold *Curzon: The Last Phase 1919–1925*, London, Boston & Berlin 1934

PECHÈRE, René *Iran: Etude de jardins historiques*, Unesco 1973

POLO, Marco *Travels*, transl. Ronald Leatham, Penguin 1958

POPE, A. Upham *Persian Architecture*, London & New York 1965

PORTER, Sir Robert Ker *Travels in Georgia, Persia, Armenia . . .*, London 1821–2

186

BIBLIOGRAPHY

POURJAVADY, N. (ed) *The Splendour of Iran*, Volumes I, II & III, Booth-Clibborn 2001

READE, Julian *Assyrian Sculpture*, British Museum 1983

ROSS, Denison *The Persians*, Oxford University Press 1931

RUGGLES, D. Fairchild *Gardens, Landscapes, and Vision in the Palaces of Islamic Spain*, Pennsylvania University Press 2000

SACKVILLE-WEST, Vita *Passenger to Tehran*, Hogarth Press 1926

——*Twelve Days*, Hogarth Press 1928

SAVORY, Roger *Iran under the Safavids*, Cambridge University Press 1980

SCOTT-JAMES, Anne, Ray Desmond and Frances Wood *The British Museum Book of Flowers* 1989

SHEIL, M. L. *Glimpses of Life and Manners in Persia*, John Murray 1856

SITWELL, Sacheverell *Arabesque and Honeycomb*, Robert Hale 1957

STEVENS, Roger *The Land of the Great Sophy*, London 1962

SYKES, Ella C. *Persia and its People*, London 1910

——*Through Persia on a Side Saddle*, London 1915

SYKES, Percy *A History of Persia*, Volumes I & II, London 1921

——*Ten Thousand Miles in Persia*, John Murray 1902

TITLEY, Norah, and Frances Wood *Oriental Gardens* British Library 1991

TJON, L., Sie Fat and E. de Jong (eds): 'Some Strip of herbage: Gardens in Persian culture'; 'The Abbasid garden in Baghdad and Samarra'; 'Botanical foundations for the restoration of Spanish-Arabic gardens'; 'The botanic garden in Muslim Spain 8th–16th centuries', *The Authentic Garden*, Clusius Foundation 1991

VALLE, Pietro della *The Pilgrim*, transl. George Bull, Folio Society 1989

WILBER, D. N *Iran Past and Present*, Princeton University Press 1948

WOOD, Frances *The Silk Road*, Folio Society 2002

WRIGHT, Sir Denis *The English Among the Persians*, Heinemann 1977

WRIGHT, Iona *Black Sea Bride*, Square One 1997

XENOPHON *The Persian Expedition*, Penguin 1949

——*Oeconomicus IV*, transl. E. C. Marchant, London & New York 1923

PERIODICALS AND UNPUBLISHED PAPERS

CHATTO, Andrew, 'Vegetation in northern Iran', unpublished papers

FURSE, Paul, FLS, 'Iran and Turkey 1962', *Journal of the Royal Horticultural Society* Vol. 87, Part 4, April 1963

GURNEY, John 'Legations and gardens, sahibs and their subalterns', *IRAN Journal of the British Institute of Persian Studies* Vol. 40, 2002

STRONACH, David, 'Passargadae', *Journal of Garden History* Vol. 14, No 1, Spring 1994

SYNGE, Patrick M. 'A plant-collecting expedition to the mountains of north-eastern Turkey and northern Iran', *Journal of the Royal Horticultural Society* Vol. 86, Part 6, June 1961

Index

I visited the gardens of Persia in 2000 and 2001 and, captivated and intrigued by their architectural simplicity, wanted to go back and study them more seriously. At the same time as these first visits, I had been learning about the history and origins of Islamic gardens for my *Story of Gardening*, which further fired my enthusiasm. I am very grateful to my agent Felicity Bryan for backing the project and to Cassell Illustrated for letting me write this book, which gave me

the chance to travel to Iran once more. I long to go back—to see yet more gardens and landscapes and to experience the kindness of the Iranian people, always ready to share carpets and *chai*.

So many people have helped me along the way and illumin-ated problems of language and history. One of the greatest difficulties has been the spelling of names. Both Sir Denis Wright and Dr. John Gurney were kind enough to correct and amend the text using a straightforward phonetic system of transliteration, but I take full responsibility for any mistakes that remain. I have retained spellings of names familiar to the reader, such as Ghengiz Khan rather than the correct Changiz Khan. Elizabeth Tucker of the Oriental Institute, Oxford, gave advice on the religion of pre-Islamic Persia. Sir Denis Wright also gave me advice and an invaluable reading list.

Among many who have helped me and pointed me toward valu-able sources are Dr. F. Ala, David Bulfield, the late Andrew Chatto, Val Dalton, Elizabeth Dickson, Ed Gilbert, Sir John Graham, Paul Ingwersen, Anne and Richard Kindersley, Mr. Peter Land, Hugh Leach, Mrs. Gazal Rouhani, Caroline Sandwich, Mr. Amir 'Ali Sheibany, Patrick Taylor, and the Director and Staff of the Institute of Forests and Rangelands.

I am very grateful to Daniel Moore of Distant Horizons and Pasargad Tours (in Iran) for arranging travel to Iran and for provid-ing Mohammad Rostami, Parisa Roustaian, Kamran Norad, and Ali Sadrnia who were excellent informative guides across the moun-tains and deserts. On my second visit to Iran, with a group and under the auspices of *Gardens Illustrated*, Susie Sanders was an asset.

I will always be grateful to Jerry Harpur who traveled to an un-known country to take his superlative photographs of gardens and landscapes. I am also most appreciative of all the hard work done

by Emily Hedges, the picture researcher. Ken Wilson, the designer, juggled pictures and text to produce a beautiful book. I owe all three a great debt.

The staff of many libraries and organizations have played a part in providing help. Norman Cameron at the Royal Asiatic Society Library in Belgrave Square, Sheila Markham at the Traveller's Club, Charlotte Tancin, Librarian at the Hunt Institute for Botanical Documentation, Carnegie Mellon University in Pittsburgh, the Iran Society and the patient staff at the British Library, the London Library and the RHS Lindley Library. Living as I do far from London the lending facilities of the London Library, which allow me fifteen books at any one time, made research possible.

My final and greatest thanks go to my editor, Erica Hunningher. Erica twice visited Iran with me and shared the excitement of garden discoveries. She has sorted out my text with dedicated enthusiasm, reading many of the same books. Without her skills and her friend-ship the book would never have been accomplished.

Picture acknowledgments

All photographs by Jerry Harpur unless otherwise credited.

Key to sources
BL The British Library; BLUO The Bodleian Library, University of Oxford; BM The British Museum; BN Bibliothèque Nationale de France; C Corbis; EH Erica Hunningher; L Louvre; PH Penelope Hobhouse; SHM The State Hermitage Museum, St Petersburg; V&A Picture Library

Cassell Illustrated and Kales Press thank the following picture sources for their kind permission to reproduce the illustrations in this book: Page 1 BL (Or.6810, folio 106 verso); 4 BLUO (cat no, 501 Arnold, p2, Pl fol 240); 8 BN (Ms.or. Smith Lesouef 198, f.1v, 2); 9 Glasgow Museums: The Burrell Collection; 14 top right and bottom left EH; 19 EH; 22–23 EH; 24 EH; 25 SHM; 32 bottom EH; 33 BL (213.4.1,Pl. 97); 35 L © Photo RMN – Hervé Lewandowski (inv. MAO 783); 36 PH; 37 EH; 39 BL (X 747, frontis.); 41 left Will Ingwersen; 42 and 43 Royal Horticultural Society, Lindley Library; 47 The Pierpoint Morgan Library, New York/Art Resource, NY. (M.500, f. 11 r.); 49 BM (WAA 118914); 50 BM (WAA 124939); 52 left EH; 54–55 courtesy of Sir Martin Gilbert, from G. Droysens *Historischer Handatlas*, Leipzig, 1886; 56 BL (646 C 2 74, Pl. LXXXIII); 57 C/Roger Wood; 58 left EH; 59 BL (646 C 2 74, Pl. LXXXXVII); 60 BL (646 C 1 74, Tome IV Pl. 216); 61 C/Roger Wood; 62–63 V&A; 64 University of Pennsylvania Museum, Philadelphia (Miniature no. NE-P-33; f.49b) 65 BL (646 C 2 74, Pl. LXXIX); 69 C; 70 C/Roger Wood; 73 Benaki Museum, Athens (inv. no 9128); 75 EH; 76 L © Photo RMN – Hervé Lewandowski (inv.K3433); 77 Caroline Washington; 80–81 John Hopkins University, The Milton S. Eisenhower Library (T.L.6 1950 ff 82V, 83); 83 BL (Or.2265, f.48b); 84 BL (Add.18 113, f. 26 v.); 86 SHM; 90 BLUO (Elliott 339); 100–101 EH; 102 top right BL (X 747, Pl. XX); 103 BL (X 747, Pl. LXXXI); 105 BL (213.4.1, Pl. 75); 106 bottom right BL (X 747, Pl. LXXX bis); 111 top right EH; 112 top BL (646 C 2 74, Pl. LXI); 112 bottom BL (213.4.1, Pl. 79); 113 The Bridgeman Art Library/The Stapleton Collection; 114 BL (X 747, Pl. XLIX); 119 EH; 120 and 121 EH; 124 BL (X 747, Pl. LXXVI); 132 courtesy of Mr. Amir 'Ali Sheibany from 'Once There Was a Town Called Tubas'; 133 top PH; 133 bottom right courtesy of Sir Denis Wright; 138 BL (646 C 2 74, PL XXXI); 140 and 141 BL (646 C 2 74, Pl.XXVI); 144 courtesy of Sir Denis Wright; 147 bottom EH; 148 bottom EH; 150–151 EH; 154 C/Ruggero Vanni; 156 Biblioteca Apostolica Vaticana (ms.ar. 368 fol. 19 r.); 157 C/Philip Gendreau; 158–159 C/Patrick Ward; 160–161 V&A; 163 C/Craig Lovell; 164 C/Robert Holmes; 172 bottom right EH;173 Will Ingwersen; 174 EH; 175 EH; 176 and 177 EH; 178and 179 EH; 180 right EH; 181 EH